THE ABSENCE OF
excess

Stories on Cultural Immersion, Godly Love, and
Living Surrendered from a Black American
Missionary in Africa

You are an Image-Bearer
God bless !

Natasha

NATASHA T. BROWN

ELOHAI
INTERNATIONAL
PUBLISHING & MEDIA

Published by ELOHAI International Publishing & Media:

P.O. Box 64402

Virginia Beach, VA 23467

elohaipublishing.com

For inquiries or to request bulk copies, e-mail hello@elohaiintl.com.

ISBN: 978-1-7348778-7-8

Library of Congress Control Number: 2020915908

All Scripture quotations, unless otherwise indicated, are taken from the Holy Bible, New International Version®, NIV®. Copyright ©1973, 1978, 1984, 2011 by Biblica, Inc.™ Used by permission of Zondervan. All rights reserved worldwide. www.zondervan.com. The "NIV" and "New International Version" are trademarks registered in the United States Patent and Trademark Office by Biblica, Inc.™

Scripture quotations marked ESV are from the ESV® Bible (The Holy Bible, English Standard Version®), copyright © 2001 by Crossway, a publishing ministry of Good News Publishers. Used by permission. All rights reserved.

Scripture quotations marked AMP are taken from the Amplified Bible, Copyright © 2015 by The Lockman Foundation. Used by permission.

Scripture quotations marked KJV from The Authorized (King James) Version. Rights in the Authorized Version in the United Kingdom are vested in the Crown. Reproduced by permission of the Crown's patentee, Cambridge University Press.

Printed in the United States of America

Endorsements for *The Absence of Excess*

"What can I say about this dynamic book and story for Christians young and mature? I am so excited about this book! Natasha T. Brown does a tremendous job not just sharing her story about her time ministering and teaching in Tanzania, East Africa, but she makes readers really think about their faith and calling. You will learn firsthand about the ups and downs of missionary work, as well as discover the joys of total surrender to the Lord. Natasha is open and honest with her feelings, but also how she was transformed by the wonderful people of Tanzania and by the grace of God. As one who ministers in East Africa, this book is <u>absolutely necessary</u> for anyone desiring to serve the Lord, especially in the Majority World. God has great plans for you to make a difference in this world and Natasha's book, *The Absence of Excess*, <u>is a must read to prepare you for His plan for your life</u>."

— DANIEL B. GILBERT, PH.D.
Director of the Masters' Program & Assistant Professor of Theology, Regent University – School of Divinity; Founder & President of EmPowered Living International Ministries; Author of *The Big Five: Discovering the Five Foundations Every Christian Should Know!*

"*The Absence of Excess* chronicles the transformational journey of Natasha T. Brown during her missionary assignment in Tanzania, Africa. The cultural differences, simplicity of life and spirit of the people she encounters, brings the author to a spiritual wakening and renewal of her faith. The vividness of Natasha's storytelling and the insights she lends in her field notes gives the reader a sense of being by her side as she teaches and travels throughout the village spreading the Gospel of Jesus Christ. *The Absence of Excess* will enlighten, inspire, and ignite the reader to embrace our Lord's mandate to the Church to, "Go ye therefore, and teach all nations.""

"The final frontier of the global missions movement is swiftly approaching. Finishing the Great Commission task to preach the gospel to all nations will actually include a more accurate missiological reflection of *all nations*. Natasha's powerful, transparent cross-cultural missions account is evidence of the growing presence and catalytic force fueling African Americans to live on mission. *The Absence of Excess* is an essential mission resource for empowerment, mobilization, and equipping, and will inspire the African American Church to tap into God's grand global narrative, boldly reaching the millions still waiting."

"As an excellent participant observer of her host culture, Natasha affirms the reality of two-way conversion of a missionary experience in her book, *The Absence of Excess*. By immersing herself in the celebration of the birth of a child and the grieving experience of losing a loved one, by giving and receiving, teaching and learning, guiding and following, the book informs the beauty of a communal life and its challenges: the degrading aspect of poverty and the richness of life in the absence of material excess. Without paternalistic attitude, Natasha has written an informative book for people who have no knowledge of the African culture."

"With anecdotes from her travels, vivid descriptions of life in a village in Tanzania, and compelling parallels to her spiritual life, in *The Absence of Excess,* Natasha T. Brown brings her readers along with her to a small farming community along the shore of Lake Victoria. Whether you are interested in missions, interested in diving deeper in your relationship with Christ, or simply want to read another book from Natasha, you will enjoy her adventures, and you can't help but learn something along the way. Pick this book up and I guarantee God will speak to you through her work."

—ASHBY RAUCH KIDD
Founder, Visible Grace, Nairobi, Kenya

Dedication

To my students at NTC: *you are special and God's plans for you are bigger than you can imagine (Ephesians 3:20). Never stop pursuing the vision he has given* YOU.

acknowledgments

To every partner and supporter of the Tanzania mission, thank you. I am grateful for your partnership. Thank you for allowing the Lord to use your prayers, love, and financial support to enable me to serve and produce fruit for the kingdom of God.

To my mission mobilizers, Christina S. and DeLoy Lance, thank you. You helped to prepare me and provided insight on Africa and missions to make my transition from the United States to Africa (and back) so smooth. Special thanks to the amazing team in Kenya: Frank and Cary Forsythe and Clarice Omungu, and all the sweet gentlemen at the Mayfield Guest House. To my Tanzania team leaders, Abram and Ashby Kidd, thank you for being His hands and feet, for being patient, and welcoming me into your home at any time, listening to my ideas, and sharing your wisdom. I continually pray that God strengthens you two as you support the region, the college, and your four sweet boys. To Rosemary Walker, your love for Christ shines through dark places and changes atmospheres—I appreciate your energy, giving, and constant enthusiasm in your service to the Lord. To the staff and missionaries of Africa Inland Mission, you taught me so much and I am forever grateful to God for you.

To Esther Nangale, Philbert Nangale, and Musa Nangale, you mean the world to me. I just pray you know how special you are. I smile (or cry tears of joy) whenever I think or speak about your family's impact on my life and how you mirror the Lord's heart. God specifically connected me with your family and I am grateful. I love you all for life – *this includes you too, Jere!* Thank you all

9

for the many adventures you led me on through the village.

Special thanks to Bishop Nungwana, Enoch Nungwana, Mary Ngussa, Alfred Ndaro, Edina and Johnson Kiula, and so many other students and teachers at NTC for your help along the way. Also, thank you to First Lady Joyce and your gracious daughter and sons, especially my *rafiki* NeStory, for keeping me company on so many afternoons and helping to illustrate my first children's book! To everyone at NTC, thank you for welcoming me into your homes and lives ~ *Karibu* United States.

To Mom, Dad, Aunt Linda, Vondra, Mac, my brother and sister Remy and Maria Brown, my sister Latoya McClinton; Aunts Diecy, Syracuse, Venetia, and Mary; Latoya Rice, Pastors Greg and Val Perry, and the Rhema Harvest family, I love and appreciate you so much – thanks for your encouragement and support and for remembering me while I was in Tanzania. To Keyonna Wallace and Felicia Biles, thank you for your friendship and sisterhood and for always supporting me during pivotal moments in my life and walk with God. I appreciate my Regent professors and mentors including Dr. Alex Mekonnen, Dr. Daniel Gilbert, Dr. Hanisha Besant, Dr. Diane Chandler, and Dr. Kimberly Alexander (and many others) for your classes, teachings, and insight. Lessons that I learned from you all were key during my time serving in Tanzania.

To Lyndon Williams, thank you for helping me tremendously with ELOHAI International and for your support in this mission! Daniel Bradley, Tokeitha Wilson, Caressa Jennings, April Fields, and prayer warriors in the Victory Prayer Circle, 10 Blessings Inspiration, and We Who Dwell, thank you for fervently warring with and for me in the Spirit!

Share your favorite takeaways or quotes on social media, and hashtag #TheAbsenceofExcess. Tag @ NatashaTBrown and @Elohai_Intl.
To join Natasha in ministry events, including Bible Studies or prayer meetings, connect with the We Who Dwell Faith Community at wewhodwell.org, on Facebook, or if you are in the United States, text DWELL to 55469.

contents

Contents

Contents

foreword

For the last five centuries missions have been unidirectional—from the West to the rest. During this time, the United States was leading the world in sending the highest number of missionaries to various parts of the world. In this noble venture, African Americans had no participation in the first few centuries. Towards the end of this historical epoch, few black American missionaries have participated through different mission organizations and through their own initiative.

There are various reasons that limited the contribution of black Americans engagement in global mission. But nothing has to do with their lack of interest, commitment, giftedness, creativity, innovation, or love for mankind or God. In science, art, sport, economy, innovation, etc., African Americans have made incredible contributions that shaped the modern world. In Christian expansion, they have untold stories too. The modern Pentecostal movement started on Azusa Street, in Los Angeles, through the son of a former slave, William Seymour. Today there are more than six hundred million Pentecostals in the world. The Azusa Street Revival was a Pentecostal gathering that occurred in Los Angeles, California, in April 1906. Most of today's Pentecostal denominations point to the Azusa Street Revival as the catalyst of the worldwide growth of the Charismatic movement.[1]

From a Western perspective, William Cary is the father of modern mission. Without going to a theological or missiological argument whether a mortal man can be a "father" of mission. If

---

1. For an in-depth understanding of this topic, see Pentecostalism: Origins and Developments Worldwide, Walter J. Hollenweger, February 1, 2005.

being first to leave one's home country and engage in evangelism and church planting in a foreign land can make one "father' of mission, George Liele, an African American, is first to leave the United States and start missionary work in Jamaica. "Thus by the time William Carey—often mistakenly perceived to be the first Baptist missionary—sailed for India in 1793, Liele had worked as a missionary for a decade, supporting himself and his family by farming and by transporting goods with a wagon and team. Apparently, he never received or accepted remuneration for his ministry, most of which was directed to the slaves. He preached, baptized hundreds, and organized them into congregations governed by a church covenant he adapted to the Jamaican context. By 1814 his efforts had produced, either directly or indirectly, some 8,000 Baptists in Jamaica. At times he was harassed by the white colonists and by government authorities for "agitating the slaves" and was imprisoned, once for more than three years. While he never openly challenged the system of slavery, he prepared the way for those who did; he well deserves the title "Negro slavery's prophet of deliverance." Liele died in Jamaica."[2]

The unidirectional missions movement is replaced by a movement from everywhere to everywhere. In this historically transformative and culturally suitable environment, even now, the engagement of African Americans in global missions is not on par to the potential and resource black American Christians have. In *The Absence of Excess*, Natasha Brown, reminds us of this truth and sheds light on the potential of the American black Christians' involvement and the impact they can make in the world.

Genuine biblical cross-cultural missionary engagement results in two-way conversions. The apostle Peter at Cornelius' house (Acts 10:1-11:18) is a good example. Peter's first missionary experience with a Gentile family, and God's unconditional salvation and the outpouring of the Holy Spirit on Cornelius' family took away the blinder from Peter's eye and changed his hatred to love,

---

2. Alan Neely, "Liele, George," in Biographical Dictionary of Christian Missions, ed. Gerald H. Anderson (New York: Macmillan Reference USA, 1998), 400-1.

rejection to acceptance, exclusion to inclusion, despise to respect, and his pride to humility. When a person engages in missionary service, he/she is putting oneself on a scene where God is a prime actor in the context of the sent missionary and the recipients of his/her ministry. As an excellent participant observer of her host culture, Natasha affirms the reality of two-way conversion of a missionary experience in her book, *The Absence of Excess*. By immersing herself in the celebration of the birth of a child and the grieving experience of losing a loved one, by giving and receiving, teaching and learning, guiding and following, the book informs the beauty of a communal life and its challenges. The degrading aspect of poverty and the richness of life in the absence of material excess.

Without paternalistic attitude, Natasha has written an informative book for people who have no knowledge of the African culture. Even if the book focuses on a local context, it reflects the general trend of lifestyle of agrarian Africans. The challenges, limitations, and frustrations, the author candidly expressed and the blessings and victories she states, affirms the paradoxical reality of cross-cultural ministry. Through weak but obedient vessels, God reveals his power and purpose.

If you think you are leading your life without purpose lack of meaning for existence, you are unhappy with all that you have, or, you want to make a difference in the life of other people and enrich your own personal life by sharing your spiritual, intellectual, and material resources, I highly recommend you read *The Absence of Excess*. It is not only mind captivating. It is educational and an invitation to engage in the global mission of God either by going or sending.

DR. ALEX MEKONNEN

Associate Professor of Missions, Regent University; Author, *The West and China in Africa: Civilization without Justice*

Notes from the Field

I am grateful for the way I see God's love in
action every day in Tanzania. In the absence
of excess, there is a beautiful place where we
find authentic community and joy for the simple
things. . . people, provision, education, rain,
and Jesus.

November 28, 2019

PART 1

cultural adjustments

a simple embrace

You never know when you are embarking on a mind-shifting, life-jolting experience until both your internal and external environments alert your senses that you have arrived. For me, that moment came after a four-day journey when I finally stepped off of the small, Precision Airways jet onto an airfield in Mwanza, Tanzania. Both the difference and similarities were immediately evident. In this place, the people who speak English often do not look like me. Those who do share my melanin sometimes smirk or laugh when I speak because my accent reveals that I am not from this side of the world. I quickly learned to laugh at myself as my new neighbors laughed at me when I attempted to speak their language, Kiswahili. That warm summer day when I stepped off of the plane from the final leg of my *safari* (journey), I was hit with a hard reality: for the next few months, I would be at everyone else's mercy—my ignorance of the language and culture put me at a grave disadvantage. I stood outside of the jet as passengers from China, Australia, Kilimanjaro, and Kenya rushed past me. I struggled to find some sense of direction, some sense of home, of knowing, of familiarity. Everyone else seemed to know where they were supposed to go while I stood on the runway staring at the signage and the different crowds of people. I followed the crowd of young Chinese men who were filing in line for a mandatory health screening before going through Customs.

Once in the line, I saw everyone pull out a yellow card as they filled out their information in a lined notebook and had their temperature taken. When I reached the front of the line, the young woman wrapped in a hijab asked for my health papers. "I don't have any," I told her. It wasn't exactly the truth. I had proof that I had been immunized for Hep-A and Typhoid Fever, but I lacked the Yellow Fever vaccination card. She scolded me through her glare, and told me to step to the side. She called her supervisor, an older, tall gentleman, who asked me why I didn't have a card. "I came from the United States. I was told I wouldn't need one."

"You stayed in Kenya for three days. You cannot stay longer than 12 hours without needing the Yellow Fever shot. You can get it here for US $500." I didn't have $500 to spend, and I quickly let him know while also giving him my best helpless girl pout and sweetest smile. He held me there for several minutes as I frantically tried to reach my contacts with the missions agency. After about ten minutes of us going back and forth, he questioning me about my plans in the country and life in the states, and after he realized I was not going to pay $500, he let me through. I knew it was God's grace and provision that moved his heart, and not those other factors. He had every right to require me to pay. With my first big challenge of getting held up at the border under my belt, anxiety, and anticipation for what the next few months held for me was in full-effect.

"What in the world have I gotten myself into," I thought.

I was embarking on a new experience that ultimately changed my life and perspective, altered my thinking, and gave me an expanded context to my faith. (As I write this section, I am still in Tanzania, so I'll share my feelings at the present moment.) I often feel like a canoe floating in a river from joy to sadness. Culture shock and transitions caused an invisible mirror to be raised before me and demanded that I look inside my soul. Immediately, I noticed my own flaws that had been masked by the excess I'd become accustomed to in my own culture. In absence of my many luxuries, I noticed the extent of my distrust for people rooted in fear of being hurt. I noticed the defense mechanisms that I had put in place that had kept me from forging deep relationships with others. I came face-to-face with the walls around my heart that forbade anyone to enter. I realized the constant questioning that went on in my mind which challenged my meager attempts at trusting others at their word, and I noticed my need to be independent, which had worked well in the world of entrepreneurship in America. But this is Africa. No one cares about my brand, business, prior successes, or personal space. No one lives in a silo, and deep relationships seem to be a way of life; I quickly learned that my way did not and do not work here. In this place, as in many African cultures, religion is not only a worldview but it is embedded into the fabric of society. In my case, Christianity was embedded in this new society and I found that how I once had to protect myself and keep guards up, here I had to work in the opposite way. I had to be discerning, but with guards down allowing myself to love first. I had to quickly shed many of my Western habits and confront my views of right, wrong, God's love, and secular living. While these were major shifts in thinking and big issues that I had to face immediately, perhaps the biggest lesson that I've learned over months of living in a village seven thousand miles away from home is the beauty of simplicity and the power of living life in the simple truth of God.

Biblical Synergy

Simplicity, love, and unexpected moments of miracles and healing describe the lives we read about in the New Testament. As a nomadic, itinerant preacher who traveled by foot from village to village, extravagance would not be an adjective to describe anything about Jesus and his disciples, except for maybe the way they performed miracles. There is a sweet simplicity that we can gather from the context of the gospels, Acts, and the epistles. As I've been studying, teaching, and hearing the Word of God, while in an East African context, it has made me rethink my definitions of *real life*, of *good life*, of *godly life*. Real life is here where people are upfront about their struggles and do not hide behind crafty captions and Instagram photos. The good life is here where my neighbors live off of the land and grow and catch food to prepare fresh with no preservatives. The godly life is here where praying for others randomly is a part of each day and people actually sing in Psalms and encourage each other with thanksgiving.

I now write this from a small village in the Busega District of Tanzania. I'm serving among the Sukuma people, in what many call "Sukuma land." Most women in this village of Bulima, Tanzania have beautiful, flawless brown skin, and the men are hard workers. My students readily pray before and after class. As you'll read in the pages that follow, people come by simply to pray with others unannounced. If you have a need that can be met by someone who hears your need they will meet it. I'm told that Christianity started in Sukuma-land when missionaries converted members of the tribe over two centuries ago. Rumor has it: Sukuma people began to take Christianity throughout Tanzania and so most, if not all the people in the Sukuma tribe are Christians. However, I also learned that there is an underworld of witchcraft and idol worship brewing beneath the surface as well. During my time working with a story group at the Bible college, I learned that some people attend church as to not be outcast, but also offer sacrifices to idols or visit witch doctors for help. This form of sorcery is not uncommon. In this and nearby villages, there is a thriving Christian community, but there are also back-sliders, Muslims, and atheists, so the people who I serve with are still committed to evangelism and sharing the Word of God with anyone who may need it and each other. Their commitment to God and devotion to the Word have truly changed my perspective of what it means to be a disciple. Add this with the classes that I taught on the books of 1 John and Romans during my second term and I have gained a totally new perspective on what it means to be devoted to the mission of God. The Bible means so much to the people who I serve among. It's really quite admirable.

The moments in times past when I stood in the middle of Times Square, New York staring at the big billboards of celebrity models and entertainers or the time I accompanied a client to Los Angeles and interviewed celebrities on red carpets, seemed like another world lived by another person—not this version of me, a missionary. In America and many Western cultures, we have so much extravagance, indulgence, and luxuries and perhaps they have become so normal that I or *we* think these excesses are what make life great. However, in Tanzania, where life is simple and few people own televisions, microwaves, or wash machines, I've learned that a godly life and the good life can be experienced when we live with little just as much as when we live with much. I'm not trying to downplay the economic disadvantages of underdeveloped countries like Tanzania, just noting that happiness and contentment are not lacking within God-centered cultures.

Moments of worship are just as relevant when the only instruments are unified voices and African drums as they are when there are electric guitars, keyboards, and lead singers. Perhaps some of us have assumed that the entire world had progressed like America beyond simplicity and crossed over into the realm of cyber, social, religious, and business over crowdedness. This isn't true. It's important for believers to expose ourselves to cultures other than our own. The West can learn a lot from the East and vice versa. Africans are not inferior and their way of life is powerful. In many parts of Africa, the culture has remained intact despite corruption, tribalism, and Europeans who Christianized and indoctrinated at the same time as they colonized and enslaved. To survive these truths and maintain a faith in God that is on fire is commendable. While many African cultures, like the one where this book takes place, may not have as many material luxuries as America, there's a simple beautiful presence here. I have found great appreciation in the farming and fishing way of life. Women still cook on firewood in the back of their houses, and luxuries that I'm used to in America simply don't exist here. However, in the spiritual sense, in many ways my friends in the village can teach Americans a lot. Here, people enjoy random fellowships and hours-long meals and conversation. Families still cherish togetherness, meals at the table, and nightly devotions into the Word of God. Church is held in small cement buildings, with cement floors, roofs, and walls, open windows and no artificial lighting or climate control. There are still many churches being planted regularly with no buildings or houses to meet. There are no big screens or smoke machines in the churches. Just the Bible, a few instruments, a podium, hymn book, old wooden pews, instruments (in some cases) and worshippers. There's a sweet simplicity about life in East Africa that must be captured. Must be savored. This is why I wanted to write this book.

I know this is a bold statement to make, but life here is closer to what I read in the New Testament than the American society from which I come. The Bible's agricultural metaphors are more than flowery figures of speech. It's not uncommon to meet fishermen, doctors, and evangelists who are sent to reach the unreached and gladly volunteer to give their lives for sake of the gospel like the Apostle Paul, Luke, Timothy, or Peter. As I've contemplated these ideas and facts, I have become convinced that the Lord would like to engage us in a simple embrace—an embrace of a life with less dependence on things, less busyness, and better relationships. An embrace which eliminates the need to be independent and instead one where we must depend on (and look out for) our fellow believers. I wrote those words, and the majority of this book, months before the global Coronavirus pandemic shook our world, but they are prophetic in nature because everyone embraced the world in a simpler way of living during this global pandemic with sheltering in place.

God wants true worshippers in spirit and in truth who will go where he sends (be it across the street or across the world), who are not so dependent on things that we can't leave everything behind for the sake of his great commission. This book is an embrace of a culture far from home and comfort. An embrace that will challenge us to worship him with the worship he desires.

The stories that follow are written from different moments during my life in Tanzania. You will experience my own spiritual journey through a cross-cultural missionary context, but more importantly, you will be prompted to reflect, and take your own spiritual journey. If my goal is accomplished, you will not only experience these moments with me, but you will also reconsider the simple truths of the Bible and become more aware of how you experience God each day. The work of the Holy Spirit is to make us more like Christ as we continue along our walks with God. I believe that he teaches us every day through simple interactions, and he guides us by placing desires in our hearts that get us to seek him more. Simplicity does not mean lacking and lacking in money and resources does not mean there is a deficiency in character and joy. This is what I hope to convey in *The Absence of Excess*. In addition, I pray that you will consider serving in a cross-cultural context. There is a lot to experience within God's many, beautiful cultures of the world. Lastly, if you have come across this book and you have yet to meet the true Savior and Redeemer of our souls, Jesus Christ, I want to encourage you to seek him for yourself and go on a journey to discover his loving nature. You will not be disappointed. The love of Jesus is the driving force behind the love that you will read about within these pages. Welcome to the layers of life and experiences that occur in *The Absence of Excess*.

a word of preparation

This book may make you laugh, cry, or shake your head. However, the main goal is to engage you into a dialogue sometimes with yourself, at other times with God, or even your own village. There will be sections in each chapter that prompt you to pray, reflect, or journal. I recommend keeping notes of your thoughts regarding each topic or chapter, but also writing to respond to the various prompts at the ends of the chapters. There is a companion journal you can purchase at my website: natashatbrown.com to help you document your thoughts. Most importantly, please pray through these sections, especially when prompted. I envision believers everywhere lifting our voices to God in prayer concerning the issues within these pages. Thank you for investing in this book and ultimately advancing God's mission on earth through your support, intercession, and love.

May God bless you richly.
Natasha

CHAPTER 1

pack light

In Luke 9:3-6, Jesus told his disciples:

"Take nothing for the journey—no staff, no bag, no bread, no money, no extra shirt. Whatever house you enter, stay there until you leave that town. If people do not welcome you, leave their town and shake the dust off your feet as a testimony against them." So they set out and went from village to village, proclaiming the good news and healing people everywhere."

I was proud of myself the night before leaving for the mission. I had managed to fit three month's worth of clothes, shoes, books, toiletries, undergarments, bug spray, medicine, hair products, you name it into one suitcase and one carry-on bag, along with one personal item, a bookbag that I'd use on the field. My goal was to be one of those missionaries with virtually no baggage. I had read about how cumbersome and annoying it could be to lug too much baggage around airports, especially while traveling the two-day journey to Africa. I had experienced nightmares where I saw myself hauling bags and bags of luggage along dirt roads in a remote village of Africa while being watched and mocked by village children. This vision terrified me. I wanted to fit into my new society. Therefore, I was patting myself on the back at my ability to pack light—that is until the moment I arrived at Dulles International Airport to find that my luggage was fifteen pounds overweight. I could have checked three bags, and yet I had stuffed everything into one and a half. I didn't have extra luggage to put the extra pounds into, so I had no choice but to pay the $50 overweight fee and continue to the gate.

After the twelve-hour flight to Doha, Qatar, I walked through immigration; I put my bookbag on the conveyor belt, and took out my laptop and other electronics. I lifted my carry-on bag onto the belt as well, then to my surprise, my clothes, books, food, and several other items fell on the floor. I rushed to pick up my things, apologizing to others in the line, while silently yelling at myself for packing too much stuff! My bag had burst open and my zipper popped. I thanked God that the airport workers at the security gate were patient with me. Unaware of the time, I took a few minutes to put together a plan. *How in the world would I travel the rest of my journey? Seven hours to Nairobi, almost three days and two locations there, then a two-hour flight to Mwanza, Tanzania followed by a ninety-minute drive to the village of Bulima?* An airport worker directed me to a cart and told me I could use that to carry my luggage.

So much for packing light.

I was lost in the airport. The huge red digital clocks around the terminal were all in military time. My Apple watch was dead, and after a failed attempt to take the cart on the airport train, I ran through the airport pushing the cart with my luggage in front of me, stopping at various stores to find out if they sold carry-on luggage. I finally found a store that had reasonably priced luggage, and before I could convert the Qatar price into US dollars, I realized (with the help of two nice Middle-Eastern women at the counter) that my boarding time was in fifteen minutes and I was at least twenty minutes away from my gate! I dropped the luggage I was about to buy and ran, while pushing the cart with my broken suitcase through the airport until I arrived at the gate to Nairobi. I couldn't take the cart through to the seating area. As I began to feel the cold flashes from the sweat-drenched attire I now wore, tears began to swell up in my eyes. I couldn't hold them back, and I was surrounded by people. "My first missions trip is starting out as a disaster," I thought as I struggled to cuddle the suitcase in my arms like an overweight baby. "Was this a mistake?" I quickly dismissed that thought realizing this was simply the enemy's way to irritate and frustrate me and throw fuel to the fire that I had initiated by NOT PACKING LIGHTLY! The sweet desk attendants at the Qatar Airlines desk assured me that I could go and purchase a suitcase. There was about twenty minutes remaining until boarding time, they said. I want to believe that God provided a divine delay of my flight that day.

At the end of this ordeal, I was able to return to the original store with the sweet Middle-Eastern women and purchase another suitcase for $80 US dollars and make it to my flight in time. I didn't think about it again, but I stored this ordeal in my head under the label, "pack light." Now, weeks later, I realize this incident was symbolic of a much more important lesson.

What type of baggage do you have?

It's bigger than suitcases and luggage. We as servants, missionaries, and Christ disciples, must always keep track of what we are bringing along on our journeys with God. Is there enough emotional space to love, show compassion, hospitality, patience, trust, and loyalty to others? Is there enough physical space to receive the new items God needs you to have for your journey? What type of baggage are you carrying? If it's too heavy or if you're overstuffed and already filled to capacity, there will be no room to be fluid, to freely give, and receive. This reminds me of another lesson I learned in hindsight. I've been an entrepreneur for many years. I have always been working on someone's project—business, book, brand, or ministry. I felt a strong press on my heart to finish all of my projects before my graduation from seminary (during the summer of 2019) and before departing for the mission on September 1. Despite that, I still found myself with more projects than I wanted to have on my plate while in Africa. I couldn't foresee the amount of *hodis* ("knocks" on the door); dinner dates; random visits with students and families; the amount of prayers for sick children; and time I'd need to spend studying and praying in order to stay nice, patient, and prepared for all that I was teaching and giving out. I managed, but had I not taken on more projects before the mission and at the end of my seminary program, I would have been able to focus *all* of my attention and energy to the ministry on the mission field. This problem has been a repeated cycle in my life. Throughout my life, I often added too much to my plate and was consequently too tired and drained to do what God was calling me to do *well* in a particular season. I was not the perfect missionary. I have often had too much baggage in various seasons of my life, including this one. I'm getting this epiphany right now (at 12:24 a.m., November 13, 2019), realizing that the timely lesson with the luggage was indicative of a bigger issue affecting my entire life. My desire and prayer is to serve God wholeheartedly without attaching myself to baggage from previous seasons. So, if I can offer any advice to you early on in this book, it would be two considerations:

1. Don't try to multitask while doing important work for God. Put your all into the one important assignment he is calling you to at the moment. (Also, realize that this is a trust thing. We often think we need to help God out by doing what we know how to do because we feel like perhaps we should be doing more. Resist this urge to over perform.)
2. Constantly assess your life and ask the Holy Spirit to reveal what is lingering from previous seasons.

Let's bring this back to having enough emotional, spiritual, and physical space to pour into God's people. It's true that we cannot pour out from an empty place, but there should be something said for being empty enough (as in willing enough) to receive all that the new culture has for us. We cannot go into new places with God attached to our existing ways while being unwilling to adapt and learn with a teachable spirit. As the Bible says, we cannot pour new wine into old wineskins. The old must go when we are entering into a new season with God.

I quickly learned that although my physical baggage fit into one suitcase and a carry-on bag, it was too much to carry along my journey. In fear, I had packed many first-world luxuries in an attempt to make myself comfortable in a third-world country. It's hard to empty ourselves, and yet I believe that it is exactly what Christ is calling us to do—to strip away our reliance on things and return to a more simple type of life. He wants us to empty ourselves from the old way of doing things, the old emotional ties to things we held onto in the previous seasons, and sometimes our old way of being self-sustainable (through business, work, or people) so that we can appreciate the still of the night, the birds chirping, the people, interruptions, and lessons awaiting us.

Take a moment to consider the things that are excessive (not just physical, but emotional "stuff"). How would you live if they no longer existed? Can you imagine the dynamics of the relationship you could have with God if these things were not around to interrupt, distract, and shape your perspectives? *The Absence of Excess* will prayerfully help you arrive at a place of deeper intimacy with the Father as you are reminded of God's simple truths of his Word and his way.

Excess Baggage Journal:

What "baggage" have you taken from previous seasons? What are you still carrying emotionally, physically, or mentally that can hinder your spiritual growth or physical elevation to your next season? How can you purge this baggage?

Notes from the Field

You don't need music here. I hear the pounds of a
drum - deep percussion.

The chants and calls of children, crickets, birds,
wild animals howling, palm leaves falling, branches
hitting against one another, red-flowered bushes
swaying back and forth. Bulima, Tanzania has its
own soundtrack.

Rich and unassuming.

September 6, 2019
First morning in the village

CHAPTER 2

anxiety, adjustments, and creature distractions

"You keep him in perfect peace whose mind is stayed on you, because he trusts in you."

Isaiah 26:3 (ESV)

My first stop on the continent of Africa was Nairobi, Kenya. I had a slight anxiety attack about thirty minutes before landing upon hearing the flight attendant's announcement that Kenya does not allow plastic shopping bags into the country. I knew this. I had "de-plasticized" my suitcases earlier that week. Although at this moment, I began to question whether or not the dozen freezer bags full of rolled-up clothes counted as plastic shopping bags. Of course they didn't, but I was nervous that something would go wrong after the twenty hours of flight time. The fines imposed for entering the country with plastic bags could be up to US $40,000 or jail time! Needless to say, I made it through customs at Jomo Kenyatta International Airport and spotted my luggage (thankful it had made it on time).

Like a nervous tourist, I waited to find someone who could let me know the next process before I went to retrieve my bag. Looking for the friendliest face, I smiled and walked over to a security guard, "Excuse me, do you know if someone will check my bag before I leave the airport?" "No normally, you will be able to grab your bags and walk right out." At that exact moment, I looked up and beyond where we were standing into the open baggage claim area was my large pink suitcase waiting by itself. I laughed to myself realizing how silly I must have looked to my angels in heaven and how God was probably laughing at me to think that he would allow plastic bags to stop this mission from going forward. "My Daddy's got me," I thought, realizing that no one was going to scan my luggage to confirm I was not a plastic bag smuggler.

Upon walking out of the airport, I saw a short gentleman, holding a white sign that read NATASHA BROWN. I knew that he was my driver from Mayfield. Still, being extra cautious, I questioned him, "Where are you from?"

Mayfield is the missionary guest house with the friendliest staff you'll ever meet. Every time I have the opportunity to stay at Mayfield, I leave with new memories and new layers to God's work through missionaries. This is the place where you can meet missionaries stationed in East Africa. Once I met a couple, with maybe five children, who served in Northern Kenya. The wife was a midwife in their village. The husband was a mechanic and builder. They taught in-home Bible studies and focused on discipleship. This couple had started a radio station that shared the gospel with Kenyans who spoke rare Cushitic and Nilotic languages. During my stays at Mayfield, I learned that missionaries are superheroes.

I watched as my driver from Mayfield loaded my suitcase on top of the silver cargo van. For my first night in Africa, I stayed with a retired, married couple, turned missionaries from the States who had been serving as leaders of the short-term missions team for the eastern region office of my agency. Their job was to train me and help me get acclimated to the culture and region over the next couple of days. We pulled up to their gated home where there was a huge, unfriendly looking dog outside (more on East African dogs later). The driver called out to another attendant on the other side of the gate. The gate opened and the husband walked out to help with my bags. It was close to one o'clock in the morning, which is probably why I would not be checking into Mayfield for the night.

In case you've never been to Africa, let me be the first to alert you about some of the things you will have to get used to depending on where you plan on visiting, living, or serving. I've never been to West, South, or North Africa so my perspectives are based on what I experienced in the East African countries of Kenya and Tanzania. I had to get used to the driver's seat on the right side of vehicles, the conservative culture which prohibits women and girls from wearing pants in the village, brushing my teeth with filtered water, boiling water to bathe when the hot water ran out, or sometimes showering in cold water, which all proved to be challenging adjustments. In Nairobi, which is a busy city that reminds me of New York or Chicago in the nineties, the traffic was unreal during the daytime. As I walked along the sidewalk to the local mall with my trainers, I learned that *piki* (motorbike) drivers often drove by and snatched purses or phones from unsuspecting foot travelers. I learned that malaria medicine is just a few bucks in Nairobi, probably ten times less than what it is in the States. I quickly fell in love with Nairobi and enjoyed communicating with the men and women I came across. I set it in my heart to return for a much longer stay one day.

Water Woes

The hot water in the home where I stayed that first night in Nairobi was activated by a switch on the wall. In the days and weeks to follow, I only wished there was a switch to turn on hot water in the village. That would be too easy. Instead, the hot water in my cottage-like duplex was solar powered. When it was hot outside, the hot water worked like a wonder. When it was rainy and cool outdoors, hot water was non-existent. During the rainy season in Tanzania, many nights I had some hard choices to make. I had to decide whether or not I would wait to shower until the next day (when there was a greater likelihood of hot water) or suck it up and wash off the sweat and dust from the day in colder than normal water. Toward the end of my missionary journey, I perfected my method of showering with boiling hot water. I would dip my washcloth in the boiling hot water that sat in a pot inside the tub and wash my entire body with a lathered wash cloth, then rinse the towel with the cold water from the tub, and then submerge my washcloth in the hot water again in order to rinse the soap from my body. I kicked myself for not thinking up this method early on. I was blessed to have water in my house and a shower and water that was hot on most days. Many of my neighbors in the village were not that lucky. Running water and solar power were most certainly a blessing.

~

Ants, Mice and Lizards

For the first couple of days at my residence in the village, I wouldn't touch much in the kitchen, because ants seemed to follow me everywhere I went. I learned the hard way that ants were very happy about my arrival after they invaded my peanut butter, granola, and chocolate that I left in the pantry. My village veteran, missionary neighbor Ashby let me know the only thing that could rid my life of these ants (or at least make life more bearable) was a super poisonous concoction called Akheri Powder. That powder worked miracles in my place after I wasted two bottles of Raid (that I'd packed from home) on chasing ants, to no avail.

The next issue that almost drove me up the wall were the lizards/geckos. It wasn't their presence that bothered me. I often chatted with friends and family via FaceTime who were completely distraught to see so many lizards crawling on my walls or under my door from outside. The presence of lizards in the village are just as common as Toyota Camrys in America. They are literally everywhere. I was fascinated by their ugly beauty. The male lizards have red heads and upper torsos with purple-blueish tails.

The females are grayish with spots. As I mentioned, it wasn't their presence that bothered me the most. It was what they left behind. These creatures used the bathroom everywhere. I would find their poop on the walls and on the floor. For the first two weeks of my village stay, this combined with the scratching noises I heard at night that sounded like a rodent running across the cement floor, convinced me that I had a mice problem. I would have bet money I did. I went to Ashby and Abram's house (they're my mission team leaders) a few times complaining to them about these mice. In her calm "I've been in this village for years, and I know there are not many mice, but I'll entertain you" voice, Ashby listened and tried to convince me that the evidence I had compiled about my mice problem was probably just "proof" of geckos instead. Again, I didn't believe her and didn't want to chance it. I just wanted to get rid of these "mice" before one crawled through my mosquito net and onto my bed at night. Ashby gave me one of her sophisticated, yet primitive looking mouse traps that she described as the "best trap ever," one that "worked every time," and I sat that trap by my back door inside of the kitchen for weeks just knowing that I'd catch the creature that was keeping me awake at night. Night one, no mouse. Night two, no mouse. Nights three, four, five, six, seven, ten, fifteen, twenty, and still no mouse. I moved that trap to another area in the tiny kitchen next to the short refrigerator, and I just knew we'd catch that sucker then. Not so. After over a month, I gave up, returned the mouse trap, and told Ashby that she was probably right. The noises and excrement that I found most mornings were most likely from the geckos. I am happy to say that I never saw a mouse in my house while living in the village, thank God.

~

Mosquitos with Malaria

Before I left for this ministry assignment, it seemed like Africa was synonymous with malaria. Everyone warned me about malaria-infected mosquitoes that are always on the hunt in Africa and the need to get a vaccination before leaving. I waited on this, and instead purchased malaria medicine at the pharmacy near the mission office in Nairobi. The price was considerably less than it would have been in the US, about ten dollars for a month's supply of medicine.

The mosquitos in the village come out mostly at night. I wore long sleeve shirts and pants to bed and slept under a mosquito net. In fact, most days, especially during the first two months, I had heat exhaustion and was extremely tired from long days, hours of teaching, visiting and praying with families, and huge meals. I was so tired that I was ready and prepared for bed most nights by eight thirty or nine o'clock in the evening. Preparing for bed meant that my front and back doors were closed, lights off (meaning no more visitors), and the kitchen cleaned. I'd shower around nine o'clock, and spend the rest of my night sitting in the bed under the mosquito net, reading, writing, studying, praying, or surfing social media (when the Internet worked). Since there is no climate control, windows have a mosquito screen and glass, but they are often left open overnight so that fresh air can flow. On rare occasions when I stayed in the living room well into the night or fell asleep on the couch, I woke up with mosquito bites on my arms, legs, fingers, or feet. For the majority of the time while I was in Tanzania, I took a generic version of a Doxycycline pill each day to prevent malaria. From what I hear, this is one of the medications (in higher dosages) that also heals malaria patients. Toward the end of my stay when I had about four months under my belt, I stopped taking the pills each day. I noticed my teeth turning yellow and fewer mosquitos inside of the house. I also realized that since I was rarely out at night, slept in long sleeves and pants, and did not hesitate to spray myself with Off!, it was highly unlikely that I'd get bitten by a deadly, malaria-infected-mosquito. I'd been paranoid for nothing. I don't want to downplay the seriousness of this disease because I know people die from malaria, especially African children, and I've been warned and have read about many missionaries who became deathly ill or died from malaria while serving on the continent. Needless to say, I protected myself in other ways from this. I eased off the Doxycycline substitute and began to take the pills one to two times a week, if that, and remained perfectly well.

~

```
Notes from the Field


Howling match between what seems to be wolves and
the dogs next door (who are barking). It went on
for about 30 seconds and stopped.
```

Friday, September 13, 2019
9:40 p.m.

Dogs that Don't Bark

My encounters with dogs challenged both my mental agility and faith. You see, where I come from, when big unleashed dogs come trotting down the street, we move to the other side of the street, stop in our tracks, or find something we can hide behind so the dogs will ignore us. Perhaps this is just a reaction based on where I'm from, but I never realized how violent stray dogs were in Prince George's County, Maryland until I met dogs who are the complete opposite in Tanzania. In the village, it is quite normal to see stray or unleashed large dogs. They stroll down the street and act as if people on the road don't exist. The first time I saw a dog, I turned in the opposite direction walking as fast as I could without running because where I grew up when you run near a dog, the dog thinks you want to be chased. So I knew I couldn't run. I started praying, then remembered that God didn't give me the spirit of fear. I gave myself that pep talk and prayed. Then, with no choices left (because I couldn't run, and I couldn't keep walking in the opposite direction of my destination) I decided to be bold and courageous and walk as if I owned the street. Do you know that after the big fuss that I put up in my mind, that huge dog ignored me, and as soon as it did, I turned around and looked as if I had just been dissed by a person after going out of my way to speak. "How dare that dog ignore me like I don't exist?" I thought. I couldn't believe that I was a non-issue to this dog. After that day, I took it upon myself to initiate a social experiment to see if indeed dogs didn't care about humans in the village. The next time a dog came strolling in the direction in which I was walking, I said a short prayer (because I wasn't sure if the previous dog was the norm or the exception) and asked the Lord to let me make it out of our encounter unscathed. The same thing happened during my next brush with a stray dog. Again, the dog walked past me as if I didn't exist. Not even a look. In fact, I think the dog turned his nose up at me and looked the *other* way! Can you believe it? I wondered if these dogs were blind, because again and again they paid me no attention. In fact, the only dogs in the village that acknowledged my existence were Thunder and Micky who lived next door. These canines often followed me home. They stood up off of their post, which was their front porch, to bark if they spotted people near their home too late or early for their liking. They barked or stood at attention often, but when they grew used to me, they would only lift their heads to see who was coming in their presence then lay back down once they realized it was me.

Soon, I figured it out: the stray dogs I encountered in the village had no intention of hurting anyone, and I took back my peace that I could have possessed all along.

The many situations with the geckos, dogs, mosquitos, lizards, and even the hot water made me realize how easy it is to welcome unnecessary distractions. We allow these distractions that are often non-issues to zap our energy. This was one of many lessons I learned in hindsight, but when we're serving the Lord on the missions field in our backyard or across the world, Satan, the deceiver tries his best to take our attention off of what matters most. As you know, in Christian work, what matters most is the time spent praying, listening to God, speaking the Word, and being Christ ambassadors. Had I spent as much time in the beginning worrying about these important activities rather than chasing mice, running from dogs, and crying over cold water, I probably could have circumvented much of the warfare that I experienced. Or at least I could have been better prepared to fight it with faith.

The scripture that comes to mind that I want to remind other chronic worriers who teeter with fear and anxiety about things they can't control is this, Isaiah 26:3:

> **You keep him in perfect peace**
> **whose mind is stayed on you,**
> **because he trusts in you.**

The "you" in this verse is the Lord. When we keep our minds on him, he fills our minds with peace. On the missions field and in life, period, there will be so many uncertainties, adjustments, and situations that arise that would like to send us into a panic. Resist the urge to fear and remember, the Lord who brought you this far is still walking through those moments by your side.

Anxiety, Adjustments, and Distractions Journal:

Reflect on your thoughts today. I challenge you to keep a journal with you. Set your alarm to stop and reflect every two to three hours. Ask yourself (and answer in writing):

- *What have you been thinking about and doing during the previous hours?*
- *How much time have you spent worrying, contemplating issues you cannot control, or stressing out over trivial matters?*
- *Is what you're doing keeping you away from service, worship, or prayer to God?*
- *How can you adjust to today's environment while keeping your mind on the Lord?*

Notes from the Field

"We create labels for ourselves that don't exist
in other cultures." - LaToya Rice

[My label: "introvert."]

October 16, 2019

CHAPTER 3

unexpected knocks

"Show hospitality to one another without grumbling."

1 Peter 4:9 ESV

Most homes in our village do not have street addresses. Besides two local *dukas* (stores the size of a very small walk-in closet), a small pharmacy attached to the house of our village handyman and engineer, and a mini market, there is no place within Bulima to purchase many daily essentials. Yet far from convenience and away from many distractions, I experienced a beautiful God-sent message from my neighbors. It was my first twenty-four hours in Tanzania, and there were several unexpected knocks at my door.

When Tanzanians hear, *"Hodi . . . hodi"* they know that someone is at the door and would like to come in. People do not typically knock on the door. They say, "Hodi," instead.

"Karibu!" (Welcome) is the proper response, often at which point the person at the door takes off his/her shoes and enters the home, upon the door being opened.

"Hodi . . ." first, around 10 a.m., my missionary team lead, Ashby, brought me dishes and came over to invite me to lunch.

"Hodi . . ." just when I began to write my lesson plan that afternoon, a young lady, who I later learned was a student of mine, wanted to know if I had the key to the principal's house because she was scheduled to clean it. Poor girl, I couldn't understand her much and she definitely didn't understand me. After a few minutes, she gave up and decided to try another house.

"Hodi . . ." another neighbor visited to sell me eggs, because he had heard I needed them. I had just closed my doors and was washing my face. I didn't realize it that day, but everyone who knocked on my door that first day would become major parts of my life in Tanzania.

In the village of Bulima, there is an open-door policy where neighbors are welcome to join you at any time of the day. I took advantage of this at one point that day and dropped in on Mary, who is the librarian at the college, an instructor in the women's school, and the head of finance. She's also the sweet neighbor who baked the dinner rolls (which they call scones) that were waiting on my table as a welcoming gift. After sitting with her for thirty minutes, she walked me around the campus of the Bible college where I met some of the students and instructors.

This community-style living where everyone is dependent and welcoming to everyone else and where neighbors embrace interruptions has me thinking a lot about my own life and the North American context to which I am accustomed.

I realized that up until that point, I had been very closed off to the world when I wanted to be. I was in control of my day's events. I owned a business and had been in school, so I lived by my Google Calendar and received a notice ten minutes in advance of every meeting or class. Here, however, the only thing that starts at the stroke of the clock are the classes that I teach, and even those often must wait until participants arrive. This all reminds me of a lesson a relative taught me when I was in my early twenties. One year, I decided to get my real estate license and join his real estate brokerage. Every day I'd come into the office and want to know what was on our agenda for the day, and he quickly reminded me of his number one rule to real estate: "We must be fluid. Things change Tashi Tash. Anyone can cancel, anyone can call, so we play it by ear." While I still prefer to stick to plans and schedule appointments in my electronic calendar that I can sync across devices, I see the point of being fluid. In East Africa, it's a must because of the event as opposed to time nature of the people here. People come and go based on events. They may have an appointment with you at noon, but if they are walking to your house and see a friend on the road who then needs a hand carrying food back to her house, and they are ten minutes away from your house at 11:55, they will walk with their friend to help carry the groceries. Once that's done, your guest will make his way to you. One event follows the next event and that is how the people here manage their time. There are pros and cons of this, but the point I want to make here is they are able to be fluid and they welcome interruptions when a neighbor knocks on the door, stops them on the street, or calls via phone.

Are you available to be interrupted at any time to do the work of the Lord? This was the question I was faced with during my first twenty-four hours in that country. The village neighbors who knocked on my door were in the process of serving and being the hands and feet of Jesus in those particular moments.

This was an important lesson for me to contemplate and live through on my first day in my new country. I wish I could say that the unexpected knocks became easier for me. To be honest, the opposite is true. Although the life of a missionary in this village is a ministry of interruptions (as one retired missionary has said), during my first three months, it grew more difficult to accept that I could not plan my time and stick to my schedule. My time was not my own. My schedule was not my own. While eating lunch, students would come over to ask me for clarification on their homework. While cooking, young girls or teenagers would come to sell fish, bananas, or tomatoes. Knocks on the door from primary school students who needed money for shoes, school fees, and hospital visits were the regular. Over the course of the next few months, these interruptions, although expectedly unexpected, became tougher to swallow. Every day I had to die to more of myself and surrender more control in order to live in and for

Christ. During my second three-month term, I learned to expect and prepare for interruptions.

I became somewhat of a professional at handling these interruptions during my second term. I would sometimes sit on my porch and work, or be proactive about meeting people at the door or outside when they were walking near the house. I'd work on the couch and greet my neighbors as they passed by. Instead of hiding and trying to maintain my definition of peace, I joined the party in a sense and made the interruptions a part of my days. On Sundays, late at night, or early in the mornings, I'd be intentional about spending time with God so that he could give me the strength for the interactions that would come later.

I want to pose the same question to you that I had to confront every day of my life as a missionary. Are you willing to answer the unexpected knocks? These knocks, I've realized, are sometimes from God. Our Father is stretching us, shaping, and molding us more into the image of his Son when he gracefully interrupts our day with an assignment to love, to be hospitable, to be giving. Have you given him permission to break up the convenience of a plan you enjoy each day for something inconvenient?

I had to realize that I cannot be an effective missionary or believer without answering "yes" to those questions. I also realized that an honest "yes" would take time. I suspect you're the same way. Let's pray for each other as we grow in grace in this area. We must surrender our need to have complete control of our own environments, yield to the Lord, and allow him to lead.

Hospitality is an important godly characteristic that gets lost in Western culture. We have so many things to do and not enough time to go deep in relationships which happens when we are hospitable.

Hospitality Prayer:

Dear Lord, I pray in the name of Jesus that you touch each reader of this message. Lord, open our hearts and make us more sensitive to your knocks. Make us more available to your call, and make us more helpful and attentive to the needs of your people. Lord, shape our hearts to welcome your children like you welcome us each time we knock. In Jesus' name, amen.

Scripture Meditation:

Hebrews 13:2
Do not neglect to show hospitality to strangers, for thereby some have entertained angels unaware.

Romans 12:13
Contribute to the needs of the saints and seek to show hospitality.

As we grow in hospitality, we will also grow in love.

CHAPTER 4

living off the land

"The earth brought forth vegetation, plants yielding seed
according to their own kinds, and trees bearing fruit in which
is their seed, each according to its kind. And God saw that it
was good."

Genesis 1:12

The Bible gives us an abundance of agriculture metaphors because in antiquity, even more so than today, land was a major resource used by God to provide and sustain for his people. The examples include eating from the land, reaping what we sow, enjoying plentiful harvest, Jesus the Vine and, we his branches, seedtime and harvest. Many people from my culture and context think of the agriculture examples as mere figurative language to describe the prosperity (or lack thereof) available to us if we work at our dreams, sow positive seeds (often thought of as money or kindness), or pay our tithes. However, living in Tanzania allows me to see these words for what they truly mean. In Genesis 8:22, when the Bible says there will always be seedtime and harvest, it is not referring to business and wealth, but the natural process of life in the spiritual and natural. There is a time to plant seed into the ground and a time for that seed to grow and produce a harvest at its proper time. Of course, we can apply this spiritual principle to the seeds we sow in business, friendships, and other areas of our lives, however, I want you to imagine these terms in the most literal way, which is why they were used so much in the Bible. The original readers and hearers of the Bible understood them as it relates to agriculture and the process by which they survived.

When I arrived in Bulima, during the dry season, the ground was brown. Dirt roads and dead grass, dry leaves, and parched palms swayed back and forth, scratching against the house to remind me of their lack of moisture. In daily chapel at the Bible college, there were prayer requests for rain—good rain, peaceful rain—enough rain to sustain the land. It was so dry and hot outside that I could barely fall asleep at night without waking up in a sweat. I remember the first day it rained. It was at the end of September, after leaving the campus in search of a game of women's netball to watch, I was walking to see little David, a missionary kid who was having his fifth birthday party. The rain blew me away. It had been so hot and dry and here it was now, RAINING showers. I ran down our dirt road, turned on my phone's camera, and started to celebrate the rain. I was so happy. It seemed as if God had heard the simple, sweet prayer requests to bring peaceful rain.

Living Off The Land

Notes from the Field

November 2019

Two months into the missionary journey and the
ground and landscape are green. Grass too high
to walk through. What were once dirt-ridden paths
leaving dust in between my toes are now patches of
green grass and mud. Pods that were uncultivated
or simply rows of neatly-plowed soil just a couple
of weeks prior are now budding with life. Rows of
maize, potato plants, rice, and beans in their
infancy stages cover the fields. I walk to and
from school and see the mamas in their shambas
(gardens) planting and digging in the soil . . .
loud noise coming down the road means I must move
to the side for a tractor trailer. More hodis at
the door . . . today there are nyanyas (tomatoes)
for sale. Sweet baby bananas or mangoes, papayas,
lemons. We eat what once grew in the soil. Their
labor and seeds sown have brought forth "fruit,"
and it's delicious. Beans and rice and corn. It was
all worth it. We live on the land . . . eat on the
land.. Earn on the land, and survive on the land.
No longer are the parables of Jesus or Proverbs
of Solomon beautiful, metaphoric pictures about
cultivation designed to only teach me spiritual
principles. This is all very practical and real
now.

February 2020

Five months into this journey and maize plants are
taller than six feet in the sky. Some have already
harvested and because of the steady, peaceful rain,
many neighbors have planted a second time. God has
blessed Bulima and anointed the ground to provide
food and livelihood to babies who once cried of
starvation.

Here, if people don't cultivate, they don't eat on a consistent basis. For many families, cultivation is not only how they receive nourishment but also a means to earn income. About seventy percent of the Tanzanian workforce engage in farming and the food they eat and money they earn is reliant on what they sow. In the village of Bulima, I imagine that number could easily go to ninety percent or more. If they do not cultivate, the family becomes dependent on those who do. The Biblical metaphors take on a different meaning when they're no longer colorful, figurative language or seemingly archaic ways of life applicable only to the first century. No, today in the twenty-first century, there are societies where people rely on the land for their livelihood. They need God to make their way prosperous. Sure, there's a part everyone plays in his or her own success and prosperity . . . weeding, planting, plowing, picking, harvesting . . . but if it does not rain . . . there's no harvest. The seeds die. If God does not make the rain fall, the people must rely on the lake or their own water, which for some households, does not exist.

~

I received a knock at the door one day that reminded me of my neighbors' dependency on God providing rain. A man who I did not know asked if I was "Nathasha" (my name is hard to say for many Tanzanians). When I said yes he gave me a white, carefully folded square, which I opened to find a hand-written note that had been folded small enough to fit in my palm. It was from someone whose name I didn't recognize, asking me to sponsor an irrigation system for his garden so that he and his family could have economic sustainability.

Not long after this journey began, I began to feel like an explorer or an appraiser, assessing the land for opportunities to create sustainability and development. I think every mission-ary and mission organization should be trained or educated to think this way when going into rural cultures. There are needs, but instead of trying to meet every need with the resources we have in our hands, we must look for ways to create sustainability that allows blessings to continue to flow after we are gone. Now, I did not provide funding for the irrigation system for two reasons: first, the cost was too high for me at the time; and second, because it would have created food security for one family out of the thousands of families in the village. I like models instead like the Bible college where I serve has implemented. They own land throughout the village and near the lake, which they enable students to rent at fairly low prices to cultivate in order to create food security for their families. As Christians, this blessing also extends outward to the village.

Before I returned to Tanzania after spending December in the States, one of my sweet sisters from church provided me with US $200 after I explained how I often gave food to neighbors. She instructed me to use $100 (roughly 231,000 Tanzanian shillings) on what she called my "food bank." I decided to take the money she gave to partner with my missionary neighbor to start a garden, which would produce squash, tomatoes, Chinese cabbage and other vegetables for our neighbors. The money helped to purchase seeds and paid for two of the gifted Bible students to serve as our gardeners (or farmers). With $100, we provided much-needed employment and food. We met two needs, actually three, because with the help of our student-workers, the land was well-kept as well, which relieved the school of an extra duty.

Notes from the Field

March 2020

We prayed for rain and now it rains just about
every day. The green is budding, and the harvest
is here. When it rains, we rejoice—no matter how
inconvenient the moist, muddy ground may be. We
prayed for this, and God is providing. I sometimes
smile walking through mud puddles on my way to
class knowing that the mud is just the proof of an
answered prayer.

~

I will not soon forget the day in September when Lucas sat in
my living room and explained that for the previous two years, he
had cultivated for his family, and for the previous two years, the
rain had come for a week or two but then it stopped leaving the
ground dry and the seeds to die. All those hours invested bent
over in the *shamba* (garden) hoeing, weeding, digging, planting
had been for naught. As he and others told me of their previous
fate how "God had withheld the rain," I told them I believed there
would be a harvest that year. And, thankfully it was. I continue
praying for the rain to bring the moisture and ripen the ground
for every society who still lives off of the land.

Please join me in praying for our brothers and sisters who need
the rain to survive. Before we pray, I also want to leave you with
a thought: though you may not be in a cultivation-based society
in an agricultural sense, you can be mindful of those who are.
Regardless of whether we acknowledge it or not, farmers are necessary. Grocery stores partner with farms and farmers to supply
produce. I want to urge you to support the farmers. Become a
consumer of local produce. Discover your local food suppliers and
shop with them directly if you can. Additionally, consider becoming a cultivator. Teach your family to garden and farm. Teach
them how others live and the processes their food goes through

before it gets to the dinner table. We need to become cultivators of the necessities that we can't live without. It's time we begin to ensure our own food security.

Food Security Prayer:

Dear Lord,

While I may/may not be in a society that must grow, catch, and raise food, I am aware that there are people in parts of the world who are. Lord, I thank you for their dedication and for gracing them with the wisdom and abilities to cultivate and grow the food that I enjoy. Most importantly, Father, I thank you for creating produce, livestock, and seafood for us to eat. Lord, I pray that you continue to provide sufficient rain in farming-based societies and enough nourishment for the living creatures over which you have given your people dominion. Furthermore, please teach your children all over the world how to grow and cultivate food. In Jesus' name I pray, amen.

CHAPTER 5

bride prices

"Make the price for the bride and the gift I am to bring as great as you like, and I'll pay whatever you ask me. Only give me the young woman as my wife."

Genesis 34:12

I was extremely distraught at the end of November when I learned that one of the young ladies who regularly attended a Bible study I taught would not be returning to school. Another student told me there was a possibility that the nineteen-year-old's parents may have received an offer of marriage for her—or that they could at any time, and if that were to happen she would have to leave school and return to her home village. Immediately, I was upset, and my mind went to the extreme: *was this teenager being sold for her family's financial gain?* There was a strong possibility that she would be getting married and would have to drop out of school and return to her home. Around this time, I had recently watched a movie set in East Africa where parents used their daughter as a means to gain wealth, cattle, and other goods. Fresh in my mind, I remembered that this movie depicted the young woman in her teens being deprived of an education in order to be a means for financial gain for her family. The young woman in the movie was unwilling and distraught, and it definitely tainted my perspective against this tradition. I had seen it in the movies, but I had not yet witnessed this issue in the village, nor had I ever considered that this was still an active practice on this side of the world. I had been naive to this tradition up until this point. I instantly wanted

63

to learn more about the marriage culture in Tanzania and quickly learned a widespread and normal practice in the country is that the groom/his family pays a bride price (referred to as dowry) in order to attain a woman's hand in marriage.

Before I go any further, I think it will be helpful to include both dictionary and cultural definitions of each term. According to my research, dowries and bride prices are different by definition. Merriam-Webster's (online) Dictionary defines *bride price* as "a payment given by or [on] behalf of a prospective husband to the bride's family in many cultures." A similar transaction is the dowry. According to the same dictionary: *dowry: law* is "the money, goods, or estate that a woman brings to her husband in marriage." The dictionary difference is that the husband or his family pays the bride price and the wife's family brings the dowry. However, in actuality, these terms are used interchangeably.

We see bride prices in the Bible. Exodus 22:16-17 reads: "If a man seduces a virgin who is not engaged, and lies with her, he must pay a dowry (some translations like the NIV say "bride-price") for her to be his wife. If her father absolutely refuses to give her to him, he shall pay money equal to the dowry for virgins." The word used for dowry or bride-price here is the Hebrew word *mahar* (Strong's H4117). The meaning is "to bargain (for a wife), i.e. to wed — endow . . ." The Swahili word used for dowry is mahari. Swahili has its origins in Arabic, hence the similarities. In the Old Testament, mahar is used this way: "to obtain or acquire by paying purchase price, give a dowry in order to obtain a wife in exchange for something." As we can see, the two terms are used interchangeably in the Bible, which is also the case in cultures like Tanzania.

Do you recall the price Jacob paid for Rachel in the Bible book of Genesis? Jacob was so enamored by Rachel that he promised to work for her father Laban for seven years in order to have her as his bride.

"So Jacob served seven years to get Rachel, but they seemed like only a few days to him because of his love for her."

Genesis 29:20

When Laban deceived Jacob and gave him Leah as a wife instead of Rachel, Jacob agreed to work for seven more years, only he also wanted to marry Rachel. A week after his first marriage, he took Rachel as his second bride and continued to work for Laban for another seven years. Later when Jacob had a daughter of his own, there was another unfortunate story which included the generational sin of deception, and there was a bride price to be paid, only this time that price was much steeper.

In Genesis 34, Jacob's daughter Dinah went to visit the women of the land where her family was staying. The ruler's son, Shechem, saw her and was so mesmerized that he took her and had sex with her. This act is referred to as "rape" in some Bible translations. Then, he wanted to take her as a wife, and he told his father to arrange the transaction. Shechem's family promised Jacob that he would pay anything to marry Dinah. The two families made a deal and the men of this land also agreed to be circumcised so that Jacob's family would become one with them. Note that there is no mention of how Dinah felt about being violated and then negotiated to be a wife (or concubine—who knows) for this man who had raped her. The men of this land were circumcised and it seems that everything would turn out well, but then we learn that Dinah's brothers were angry because Shechem had defiled their sister. The brothers killed the men of the town while they were sleeping and took their goods. In this case, the price for raping Dinah (although the man wanted to marry her) was death. Aside from this rather gruesome narrative, in the Old Testament, we see that bride prices and dowries were a way of life.

In Tanzania, men pay bride prices for their wives-to-be and it can be in the form of Tanzanian currency (shillings) or livestock. I was even more agitated by this when I learned that one of the factors that increase or lower the price of brides is the color of their skin. Lighter skin is worth more than darker skin. I was hit with the cold, hard truth that the damaging effects of slavery (resulting in colorism) still affects Africa, just as much as it affects African-Americans in America. I grew more grieved when I heard Tanzanians refer to lighter-melanin Africans as white, although they are visibly black. In my opinion, by referring to light-skin people as "white" instead of light-skin, these individuals are being robbed of their blackness, while the culture perpetuates the idea that black people in Africa can only have darker hues. The Swahili word Tanzanians use for light-skinned people is *mweupe*. The English translation of this word is "white," but, apparently, the connotation in Swahili is "light-skinned." Whereas, the word that Tanzanians use for Caucasian people is *wazungu*. Interestingly enough, I was also referred to as a *mzungu* (singular form of wazungu) when people learned that I was from America. I realized, however, by talking with my friend Loyce from the village, many Tanzanians have never met a black person from America nor did they realize that there are black people in America. I posted a conversation with Loyce and I on my Instagram TV channel, which was really popular.[3] I was extremely disturbed that light-skinned black people are referred to as "white." It put me in the mindset of white-washing and forced conformity from the colonizers and slave traders who attempted to rob our identities as black people in the first place. We've digressed from the topic of bride prices, but I just want you to understand how I began to learn many facts about this culture that simply visiting for a few days would not have afforded. I am not claiming that I have all answers or even the correct perspective about how things are in Tanzania. This is, however, my perspective. I grew to love and respect many aspects about relationships and marriages in Tanzania (which I discuss later in chapter fourteen), but the issue of bride prices is one that triggered me from years of working on behalf of domestic violence, sexual abuse, and sex trafficking survivors.

---

3. Natasha Brown (@NatashaTBrown), "Are there really black people in America?" Instagram TV video, November 18, 2019, https://www.instagram.com/tv/B5BSFRzBFju/.

An unspoken influence that seems to still permeate the culture is colonialism. Tanzania was colonized by the Germans in 1884 and then the British took over in 1919. Tanzania, which was called Tanganyika became independent in 1961 and gained its republic status in 1962. Zanzibar (which was not a part of Tanganyika) gained its independence in 1963. After some violence, Zanzibar and Tanganyika merged to become Tanzania. Christianity was introduced to Tanganyika between 1505-1513 by Roman Catholic Franciscans.[4] During the same time period missionaries began evangelizing here, indoctrinating Tanzanians in their way of life. In many respects, European influences are still very prevalent in the Christian community in Tanzania. The English songs that are sung in churches (within the denomination I served) come from hymnals from the mid-twentieth century. These influences also exist in doctrinal beliefs, and even the thinking regarding lighter skin. The culture is also heavily influenced by Arab and Chinese cultures. Bride prices are still very much a part of their society, and people marry young when possible. Some of the views about skin color are oppressive. A higher bride price is applied to lighter-skin women (although other influences affect this amount as well), and this perpetuates the idea that light is right or at least better. It is the "field negro verses house negro" slave ideology.

Again, I'm no expert on Tanzanian society, and I write this humbly, but honestly from my own perspective. I share this to raise awareness about a culture on the opposite end of the world, one that I love and respect, but with certain traditions that I do not necessarily understand or agree.[5]

---

4. "Tanzania Religion," East Africa Living Encyclopedia, African Studies Center University of Pennsylvania, last assessed September 9, 2020, https://www.africa.upenn.edu/ NEH/treligion.htm.

5 Here are some additional links to background about bride prices in Africa:

Dr. Y, "Bride Price Practices in Africa," African Heritage, January 5, 2018, https://afrolegends.com/2018/01/0/bride-price-practices-in-africa/.

"Bride Price Practices in Africa," BBC News, Last modified August 6, 2015, https://www. bbc.com/news/world-africa-33810273.

Prayer for Women and Understanding:

Dear Lord, right now I come to you in the name of Jesus praying for the women and girls in Tanzania and cultures around the world. I pray for their equality, equal rights at education and business, and that they would be afforded the same opportunities as men. Lord I pray that the color of their skin, familial background, or their education do not serve as hindrances to their futures. Lord, furthermore, I come against every form of twenty-first century slavery and oppression against women in the name of Jesus. I pray that people on the outside looking in will be open-minded and gracious when learning about cultural issues concerning gender and relationships. God please give us your perspective. In Jesus' name, amen.

CHAPTER 6

single, female, african-american missionary

As soon as I arrived on the continent, I found the brochures, missionary marketing, and videos to which I had been exposed to prove true: as a single, black American missionary in East Africa, I was indeed the minority because of each of those distinct characteristics. Fewer singles enter the mission field than married couples. Far fewer African-Americans (or Black people from any country) serve as cross-cultural missionaries in Africa compared to our European counterparts. And far more single women enter the mission field than single men. While I did not become a missionary to meet a spouse, learning the reality of these facts made it clear why being a single female missionary is a topic of research, discussion, and often a hinderance among those called. My marital status, gender, and nationality were topics of conversation and sources of exploration for myself and those around me as well.

Serving in Africa as an African-American

North American missionaries began to contribute to philanthropic efforts in Africa during the early nineteenth centuries, and their involvement in Africa peaked, like most European missionary efforts, during "the heyday of European colonialism between the partitioning of the continent in 1884-1885 and the onset of decolonization in the 1960s."[6] African-American missionary presence

---

6. Elisabeth Engel, "The (African) American Missionary Movement in Africa

was pioneered in the African Methodist Episcopal Church, which was the first church denomination in America founded by Black people.[7] Black protestant missionaries had a strong biblical focus that directed their interests toward Africa as a mission field. There were also many who believed that God's providence had brought Africans as slaves to America so they could return to evangelize Africa. This history is little-known and due to the limited presence of Black American missionaries in Africa, compared to Europeans, it's often overlooked. Researcher Dr. Elisabeth Engel of the German Historical Institute in Washington, D.C. has noted that despite multiple efforts from the Black church in America, which has sent missionaries to Africa, "none of these initiatives resulted in enlarging the African American missionary presence in Africa. Estimates have it that their number totaled about 600 between 1820 and 1980, which is exceedingly small if compared to the about 30,000 American missionaries who worked in Africa in the same period." [8] *The Journal of Religion in Africa* notes:

> Over a period of 150 years African American missionaries sought to spread the Christian Gospel in the 'Black Atlantic' region formed by the Americas, Africa and Britain. Relatively few in number, they have been largely ignored by most historians of mission. As blacks in a world dominated by persistent slavery, ideas of scientific racism and also by colonialism, their lot was rarely a comfortable one. Often called, by a belief in 'divine providence', to the Caribbean and Africa, when employed by white mission agencies they were invariably treated as second-class colleagues. From the late 1870s new African American mission bodies sent men and women to the mission field. However, by the 1920s, black American missionaries were viewed with alarm by the colonial authorities as challenging prevailing racial ideas and they were effectively excluded from most of Africa.[9]

in the Early Twentieth Century," August 29, 2017, http://www.processhistory.org/engel-american-missionaries/.

7. Ibid.

8. Ibid.

9. David Killingray, "The Black Atlantic Missionary Movement and Africa, 1780s-1920s," *Journal of Religion in Africa* 33, no. 1 (2003): 3-31. Accessed August 30, 2020. http://www.jstor.org/stable/1581633.

Though years removed, this was the backdrop for me as I entered Tanzania as an African-American missionary. Other missionaries within this organization would meet me and confirm if I was in fact a volunteer with our specific mission noting that I was one of few African-Americans serving with the mission in Tanzania and at all. God led me to serve with this organization, and I loved their focus on Africa, the variety of positions available, rich history, and support provided by the US team. It didn't matter that I would be a minority in terms of my skin color. I did not realize at the time that as a missionary with this specific organization, my duty would be to prepare disciples and ministers to serve within the denomination first established by missionaries from the organization in which I served. Although now, the denomination acts as independent apart from the mission agency, much of the traditions from early missionaries still influence the church structure, traditions, and thought processes.[10]

On Fridays, when I traveled to Mwanza and spent time in a coffee shop where other expats convened, I met mostly Caucasian volunteers with NGOs or church organizations from Canada, South Africa, the US, and the United Kingdom (UK). Not until the week of my departure did I connect with another African-American female missionary who was serving in the same Tanzanian denomination and in the same region as me. She and I learned that we also attended the same graduate school in Virginia. In comparing verbal notes with her, I learned that my experiences as a single, African-American, female missionary were not isolated.

I learned that not many Tanzanians in this region had ever met African Americans before. (Those who were involved in business or had been educated were more widely exposed to American culture and people than those who solely focused on farming, church, and home life). Though the missionary presence had been strong, and they were grateful for the contributions of missionaries who

---

10. This includes views about the role of women in the church, who serve as evangelists and missionaries, but not pastors or bishops.

had helped build schools, train teachers and students, establish sustainable farming methods, provide healthcare, and much more, these volunteers had been primarily Caucasian. Upon meeting my black missionary sister who is also an educator, I was proud to know that although our presence was scarce, we had a presence. Not that our race should determine our service, but in the greater missionary culture, it is rare to hear of African Americans serving long term in a culture away from home. She has been serving in Tanzania for different seasons and assignments since 2017.

While I've heard many Black people share a desire to travel to Africa as a way to "get back to the motherland" or be "with our people," or even "serve our people," I found that although I felt that solidarity and a nostalgia with being in Africa, the visual differences in my appearance in addition to my status as a Black American missionary, caused me to stand out in the villages.[11] Even though my skin color was the same as my neighbors, my thick hair, American accent (especially the lack of fluent Swahili), makeup, and clothes I wore gave away the fact that I was not from Tanzania. Most women and girls cut their hair short or they wear braids. My hair was often big and curly or straight. My appearance caused confusion for many people. I grew used to children stopping on the roads to stare at me or older men and women pulling my hair or commenting on my appearance. I did not try to be glamorous there, but one missionary from Canada pointed out that my small cross necklace, watch, cell phone, and hair were enough to make it appear as if I was a rich American. The last thing I wanted to be known or viewed as was a rich American.

Unexpectedly, my marital status made me an anomaly as well, and the genuine desire for many of my neighbors to see me married and as a permanent fixture in the village was both flattering and troublesome at times.

---

11. I did not stand out due to my appearance much in the city as many women wore longer hair and both men and women were more westernized.

Being a Single, Female Missionary

One morning, about five months into this mission, I laid in my bed praying through the book of Ephesians and came across chapter three verse twelve: "In union with Christ and through our faith in Him, we have the boldness to go into God's presence with all confidence." In my bold confidence, I asked the Lord, "How long do I have to wait to get married?" This was after a week of intense spiritual warfare, and I felt inclined to take everything to the Lord. I had a moment with God that I will tell you about shortly, but first, I would like to alert you to a "thing" on the mission field that I did not consider before entering.

"Singles, mission work takes strength — more than you know, but not more than God will give you."

—Mike Delorenzo, Africa Inland Mission

According to recent numbers from mission agencies and boards, two-thirds of active missionaries are married couples; one-third are single women, and the rest are single men. That comes to about eighty percent single women to twenty percent single men. According to Africa Inland Mission, of every ten single people sent to the mission field, only two are men.[12]

Thankfully, I didn't know or think about any of these things before I went to Africa, and I learned the hard way how lonely it can get on the mission field, especially when you don't prepare for your singleness to be a thing. At times, I felt like a complete anomaly being a single, female missionary from America. People asked, "How old are you?" "Why aren't you married yet?" "Do you want a husband?" or worse, "Why don't you want a husband?" "What if your husband wants to do something different than you?" "Will you still come to Tanzania after you get married?" "Would you marry a Tanzanian?" Some even thought I'd be eager to accept marriage proposals from men simply because I was single or they

---

12. John Piper, "Why are Women More Eager Missionaries?," Desiring God Episode 982, December 28, 2016, https://www.desiringgod.org/interviews/why-are-women-more-eager-missionaries.

were single. Also, some automatically assumed I was a potential wife for any single man in my age group. I learned that those assumptions are a part of the culture. I write more about this later, but I found that Tanzanians aren't complicated when it comes to marriage, which was a beautiful realization. It may not be easy being a single, female missionary—the field is challenging, gets lonely—but God has called many single women of years past and he continues to call us to the mission field today. In exploring this topic, I found several articles and online forums. In a post on *askamissionary.com*, one reader wrote: "Are single women missionaries accepted in third-world countries? Married women without children?" A veteran missionary offered the following response, which I would like to echo here:

> "Single women are more readily accepted in some cultures than others, but just as with everything else on the mission field, it comes through relationships. More than once I have had total strangers (men and women) ask me such things as, "Don't you want to be married?" or "What's wrong with you that you don't have a husband?" If you are confident in the Lord's call on your life and that for this time (or forever) he has you where you are, others will accept that, too."
>
> —Betsy, who served with Send International for twenty-three years, primarily in Spain[13]

Of course, I didn't think about any of these truths before I answered the call to become a missionary. I just wanted to fulfill God's purpose for my life, like most missionaries. I wanted to be an obedient and faithful Christian who advanced the great commission. I wanted to lead people to Christ or disciple those who were young in faith. I wanted to obey God. I had been in divinity school for three years prior, and for the most part during that time, while I prayed that God connect me to my purpose partner in the form of a husband, I was also not consumed with it. I

---

13. "Are single women missionaries accepted in third-world countries? Married women without children?," Last assessed August 15, 2020, https://www.askamissionary.com/question/564.

was totally satisfied and fulfilled in my singleness. I wasn't lonely nor did I feel like my life was lacking. In Africa, however, things changed. I started to feel like I wanted a husband more than ever. I had not been prepared for the issues that would come along with my singleness on the missions field: the loneliness, difficulty communicating with natives, and limited people who understand the dynamics of being a missionary in Africa. Nor did I account for the spiritual warfare that I would face because of it. As I have been writing this book, I have had to circle back to this section on singleness several times and ask myself "is it really relevant to the purpose of this book? Will my readers be able take anything from this discussion?" I've decided to leave it in for the simple reason that if I can forewarn another single missionary what to expect and the type of challenges he or she might face as a non-married person on foreign soil, it will have served its purpose. Depending on the country and context that you serve; your assignment; whether you will live in a village, city, or countryside; and the customs and traditions of the ministry context; your world as a cross-cultural worker will be different from mine. I served at a Bible college in a village unlike most surrounding villages, in that we had certain advancements because we were at a college. I was far away from a major city and it wasn't easy to get most items, yet I was also near other missionaries who regularly voyaged into town. I was in a traditional and conservative context where women did not wear pants and marriage was the desired goal and expectation. Most people outside of the immediate school community spoke a different language than me and did not know how to communicate in English. I learned a little Swahili, but this was a major source of my problems, frustrations, and isolation. Side note: I highly recommend learning as much of the language as possible regardless of the time you will spend in a foreign country. No matter how long or short your visit, knowing a little of the local language will go a long way.

As feelings of loneliness and isolation set in as I went

blow-for-blow with the devil who tried to suck me into his mind games, I started researching to learn more about the phenomenon of single missionaries to see if I was alone in my feelings and experiences. I came across some helpful articles and tips that I want to share for anyone who finds themselves in a similar situation as me. The International Mission Board (IMB) suggests the following helpful advice for singles considering overseas mission work[14]:

Study what God says about singleness in Scripture. Carry it in your heart so you can quickly recall it on days when you feel like an outsider in the Christian community.

- Being married with children is probably wonderful. But it is not everything. Don't idolize marriage and children if God leads you down a different path.
- Read biographies of other single missionaries. Lottie Moon, Amy Carmichael, and Marie Monson are a few examples. Focus on the spiritual characteristics and personality traits that helped them thrive.
- Examine it carefully, but do not suppress the call of God in your life.
- Let eternity guide your thinking. This temporary existence on earth prepares you for an eternal dwelling that matters so much more than your marital status.
- Do not waste a single day wishing you were living someone else's life.

I would add to this list to spend as much time with God while you're on the field. Although it can be difficult to pull away from ministry, your strength, confidence, and peace will pour out of the secret place with God. During the height of the spiritual warfare I experienced, a friend proposed marriage to me, and this added another level of attack on top of what I was already experiencing. Of course God did not tell me to marry him, but I found myself questioning, *"Am I being shallow?" "What if I'm supposed to stay in Tanzania?" "Maybe I am not hearing God clearly and this really is*

---

14. Emily Stockton, "If Mr. Right Never Comes Along: A Single Woman on the Mission Field," IMB, September 5, 2017, https://www.imb.org/2017/09/05/single-woman-mission-field/.

my husband." I sought counsel despite knowing in my heart that this potential marriage was not God's plan for our lives. It was a very difficult time and I truly desired to meet my soulmate. I often wondered if God had called me to live as an overseas missionary and if he would allow me to live this life without a husband.

I started this section by sharing part of an experience I had in prayer, boldly asking God to reveal facts to me about my husband, I asked the Lord, "How long do I have to wait to get married?" He began to answer me in his mysterious way. While I won't share the details of everything he spoke to me in prayer that morning, I will say this, while it may not be easy to view our lives from God's perspective, God reminded me that we should keep his kingdom in mind in all things (Matthew 6:33). I thought I was simply praying bold prayers from a frustrated place, and asking God for big answers when I prayed about my husband and marriage that morning. However, God spoke to me in a way that I could understand him, letting me know that his ways are not my ways, and his time is not my time. He showed me that part of the reason for this wait and why I needed to be patient with my marriage is because he is still making me and my future husband fit for the purpose we will carry out together. Remember, kingdom marriage is about fulfilling a specific God-ordained purpose.

If you are waiting for *the one*, keep serving and continue to live a missional life, surrendered to God while you do so. I know God wants to produce kingdom marriages, but he is more concerned about establishing his kingdom on earth. In order to have kingdom marriages, we must be kingdom-minded singles. So whether you're serving the Lord at home or abroad, whether you're twenty-three or seventy-three, and whether you're a missionary, minister, or servant leader to your family, do not lose sight of God's will or lose hope in a marriage that honors God. Live missional now, so that you have a vision for the mission you will carry out with your spouse. Remember that your marriage is not about you or God's desire to make you happy. It is about the kingdom and

God's business to bring souls into relationship with him.

Not every person is called to be married. However, I do believe God knows and honors our hearts' desires as long as we delight ourselves in him and our desires are in line with his will as revealed through his Word.

"Take delight in the Lord, and he will give you the desires of your heart."

Psalm 37:4 (NIV)

More missionaries are needed in God's harvest, and the harvest is always God's main concern—continue to focus on that. Be a missionary and mission-minded disciple whether you are single, married, or living at home or abroad.

If you're considering a life of service to God, don't allow any of these factors to dissuade you from serving in Africa or anywhere for that matter. In fact, I pray that the opposite is true. I pray that you ask the Lord if he would open a door for you to become a missionary in Africa. If you are entering foreign soil as a missionary, lean in close to God so he can be the provider of all things that you need. Remember that you are called. You are worthy, and you are not inferior due to your skin color or marital status. We need more representation from Americans (Caribbean, Canadians, etc.) of color in Africa. Our shared, yet varied, experiences will do so much to inform our thinking and the global empowerment of Black people in Africa and beyond. While this chapter is just a drop in the bucket of issues, research, and information you may need to inform your decision-making as one who goes, sends, or prays for missionaries, I hope that it has at least inspired you to think or dig deeper into the issues affecting global missionaries and your specific role.

Mission-minded Reflections and Journal Prompts:

- *What factors are influencing your decision to serve God and your complete surrender to him?*
- *Have you ever found yourself saying, "I will serve God when_____" or "I want to become a missionary when_____."*
- *Do you consider your skin color a factor in your service to God and the specific context to which he has called you? How would you respond if you realized that it was a factor to others?*

CHAPTER 7

God filling for spiritual warfare

In November of 2019, two months into the mission, the enemy started launching fiery darts at me daily. Sometimes, I'd be so tired, or irritated, or apprehensive about having yet another conversation with someone who did not understand me or them me. I was tired of feeling guilty for saying "no" to requests for things that I could not give. My identity had taken a hit, badly. *Who am I and why am I here? What will I go home to? Will I even be relevant anymore?* I was caught in the middle of two worlds, and due to the depression, worry, or weariness, I had started to isolate myself after mandatory ministry and teaching engagements each day. On top of all these questions and worries, I had a huge decision to make: would I extend my time on the mission field and return in January or figure out my new life in the States after having graduated from seminary, moving out of my apartment, and packing my belongings into storage and a car before coming to Africa?

Tuesday, November 12, 2019

On this particular day, an author with my publishing company texted me and said, ". . . . You're doing kingdom work! You're a ministry in itself! We're praying for you and I pray you have a prayer partner in the moment the enemy speaks so that your prayers and faith yell!"

After receiving his text, I wrote the following in my journal:

His text encouraged me, but it made me realize
that I did not have [a prayer partner]. (And the
enemy has been speaking A LOT.) When I was home, I
had a roommate who prayed with me. A prayer group,
fellow seminarians, prayer calls, a church family.
We had Friday night soaking prayers and Monday
morning School of Divinity prayers. Intercessory
Prayer before church on Sunday and Bible study
Wednesdays, Thursday prayer calls, and friends who
would pick up a FaceTime to pray immediately. But
in Africa, on the mission field, most of that is
gone. Different time zones. People are busy. My
posts make it seem like I'm OK . . . like I don't
have moments when I yearn for the familiarity of
home or for prayer warriors and partners. Sure we
pray a lot here, but there is no one that I can be
transparent with. If I really shared my PERSONAL
prayer requests in public at chapel or Bible Study,
I would probably be judged and talked about.

November 12, 2019

9:48 p.m.

You can probably gather that I felt like I was all alone. Reading
this entry reminds me of the prophet Elijah in 1 Kings 18 after he
defeated the 450 false prophets of Baal. Queen Jezebel then waged
an all-out attack on his life. Elijah fled a day's journey and stopped
in a cave where he wished he could die. He thought he was all alone
and that he was the only prophet of Yahweh remaining amidst the
others who had bowed down to the idol Baal. God soon let him
know that he was not alone—others had been preserved as well.

This time period was the climactic point of spiritual warfare
I experienced in Tanzania. Looking back on it, I believe it was a
strategic attack from Satan to keep me from renewing my assignment and returning to the field in January. Perhaps the devil
thought that if I became so weary, sad, worn down, insecure, and

exhausted (I felt all of this) from his attacks, I would have tapped out and quit. I had to make a decision on whether or not to return and I needed to do it quickly so I would be able to secure my teaching schedule for next term and raise financial support. In my heart, I knew God was calling me to return, and therefore my faith history and the Word of God told me that God would provide. However, discerning God's will (from personal desires) becomes difficult when there's clutter and turmoil going on in your mind. Before I go on, let me give you a word of caution. **Whenever you have a big kingdom decision, gird yourself up with prayer and fasting and stand in faith if you begin to experience attacks. Don't abandon your assignment because of temporary opposition. The Bible tells us to submit to God, and resist the enemy, and he will flee from us (James 4:7).**

The attacks on this particular day were bouts with my identity and depression. I was also still basing my identity off of a former season of my life, when God was doing a new thing. It's very important that we learn to discern the times and when seasons are up! Life in Tanzania is much different than what I had been used to and so was the worship life and style. No soaking prayer, prophetic meetings, or the spiritual charisma that I grew to love in Virginia Beach for the previous three years prior to this. I missed home badly. I also felt like an anomaly because the Christian tradition here did not operate openly in the five-fold ministry; no one else spoke in tongues, or would lay hands and pray in faith for miracles. I desperately missed home.

The Remedy

A few hours after I wrote the post above I found myself deep in prayer, deep in the Word of God, suddenly fighting off sleep like I did most nights simply to spend more time in the presence of God. I am not trying to be spiritual, nor do I want to sound super holy, but I'll be honest. I desperately needed God at that moment because I had reached a breaking point and all I wanted to do was to crawl under my covers and become invisible. On this particular night, I cried for the first time while on the continent. I felt so lonely and forgotten. But then something amazing happened. God used that author, someone I never would have expected, to send an encouraging text that gave me fuel for my life, mission, and God's call. During our message exchange, he also sent me an article with scriptures that helped me go deeper in prayer. As I read that article and meditated on the scriptures, I realized that God wanted me to seek him in that empty moment so that he could fill the voids. Just like in the case of Elijah, God showed up in a still, small voice and began to give me a more accurate picture of what I was facing.

For days I had been sulking in my inadequacies and beating myself up over my deficiencies, which made me angry. Despite feeling unworthy of being a missionary, I told myself things like, "I am not as holy, as knowledgeable, as financially well-off as other missionaries." I knew God had called me there and I felt like he was calling me to return. Of course I did what most of us do when we are mad at our own insecurities: I looked outward. I blamed other people: not vocally, but inside I thought, *I don't have anyone praying for me. No one cares about me. I'm all alone. No one texts or FaceTimes me just to see if I'm okay. Everyone has forgotten about me.* I blamed others for the voids I felt. I was mad that I had no one to be transparent with, when in reality, I needed to be honest with God so he could hold the mirror up to me then bring me in close to him.

Most often when we are angry with others for not loving us like we desire or not calling us as much as we'd want, not praying for us, or checking in, truly we need to lean in to the Father so that he can fill our voids.

As I spent time with the Lord, I received a fill-up that night, and I woke up early the next morning to get some more. After spending the time I needed to with God, everything else flowed easily. I walked to class while worshipping along to some of my favorite gospel music songs. I prayed for my class with ease. I taught about justification through Christ by faith with ease. I sat through chapel and then worked in the library with ease. I interacted with other missionaries with ease. I engaged in my Swahili lessons with ease, and I hosted guests for dinner that evening with ease. No more striving. God filled me. He wants to fill us each day, but it requires getting rid of the excess: turning off the distractions, tuning out the voices, letting go of the self-criticism and doubt, and remembering that we have enough. We are enough. And in my case, even if I couldn't bring the spiritual community I had in the States with me to Africa, even if I didn't have a human prayer partner whom I could call when the devil talked, I *always* have a prayer partner in Jesus who sits high and makes intercessions for me daily. We have all we need and there are no deficiencies when God becomes our filling. (Let me note that I had to realize that God had allowed me to be consumed with him in a community like that in Virginia Beach so that I would be able to pour out in this and later seasons.)

Sometimes, our worship or service for God can become idols. We seek spiritual experiences instead of encounters with God. We become hooked on serving him instead of being hooked on him. I believe that in the absence of excess, when we don't have many distractions taking us away from the relationship God wants to have with us, we get an opportunity to cultivate that relationship and experience God in the simple beauty of his creation—like nature and other people, or his Word, his works, and his ways. God is all around us and in us. We don't need spiritual experiences to fill us up when we have a true, pure relationship with the Father.

Healing in Spiritual Warfare

In the absence of excess, we can reflect and notice our inadequacies, our idols, and our desires which then give us an opportunity to surrender and take ourselves to God to be healed. Sometimes, our society talks about healing like it's a one-time thing, like we can snap our fingers and be healed or go through a process, counseling, self-help books, purging, a spiritual conference, church, and voilà, we have received our breakthrough. However, I've learned that healing happens every day for those who are honest and who can feel. We all feel the effects of this broken, sinful world daily. We experience sadness, grief, loneliness, disappointment, inadequacy, fear, pride, and a lack of confidence—maybe not all at once, but some of these emotions are bound to creep in. These are all effects of the fall of humanity (Genesis 3) that represent brokenness and require some sort of healing balm. It's called being human. People who don't feel these things are probably, one: masking their feelings with dangerous and illegal substances; two: they've been through so much hurt that they've become numb; or three, they do not walk with God or are narcissists. Once we are filled with the Spirit and have joined the family of Christ, we naturally suffer through these emotions and moments, just as Christ suffered. Believers who are serious about this walk with God can experience that healing by sitting at the feet of Jesus. Unfortunately, there is a large part of the population around us who do not know how to be still in God's presence and receive his healing balm. These people walk around frustrated, angry, bitter, or they seem fine, but are secretly covering up the years of pain and brokenness. I've been one of "these people" and I had often fallen back into the rut of not feeling like I could pray or hear from God, or I was too distracted to sit at his feet. When it gets like this for me, I'm honest with God: "I need you right now, Lord, but I feel far from you. Help me Jesus." It often takes me worshipping and putting my mind back on Jesus and off of my problems, but as soon as I do, I can sense God's peace take over me. I know that he is healing me.

At other times, I pray in the Holy Spirit (tongues) to worship and talk to God. Praying in the Holy Spirit builds our faith (Jude 20). I realized during my second mission to Tanzania, that I had allowed the spiritual warfare and condemnation of my spiritual practices to get to me. I had not been using my personal prayer language, which is a weapon, as much as I had before going there. I realized that although I often found myself teaching about and explaining the gift of speaking in tongues, I had been failing to use it personally as a tool for worship and warfare. One day it hit me like a can of bricks. God had given me a secret weapon. That night, I committed myself to praying in tongues for a great deal of time. It edified me. I praised God in tongues, and I felt a release from the heavy spiritual attacks that I had been under for quite some time. God used this gift to fill me with his spirit and give me strength.

If you feel the impact of the brokenness or loneliness around you, you are not alone. It's so important to get alone with God, cry out to him, and share your feelings in the secret place. Cut off the phone, lock the door, and tune out every voice you hear. He has your answers.

Clarity after Clutter

By the time this mini-crises ended (the one that I talked about at the beginning of this chapter) and God filled me with his truth, I decided to renew my time in Tanzania and return to teach the following term. In his book, *God's Generals* Roberts Liardon writes, "Praying in other tongues will birth the will of God in your spirit." That's exactly what happened to me. In hindsight, I know this was a strong attack waged by the enemy to keep me paralyzed and unconfident about my ability to serve. He wanted to stop what God had planned. He wanted me to abort the mission. I received clarity after the clutter.

Many times when we are desperate for a God filling it is because the enemy has waged war on our minds or on our assignments. In those instances the only way to fight and win is to armor up (Ephesians 6) and connect with God's Word and will.

Ephesians 6:10-18 reads:

> **Finally, be strong in the Lord and in his mighty power. Put on the full armor of God, so that you can take your stand against the devil's schemes. For our struggle is not against flesh and blood, but against the rulers, against the authorities, against the powers of this dark world and against the spiritual forces of evil**

> in the heavenly realms. **Therefore put on the full armor of God,
> so that when the day of evil comes, you may be able to stand
> your ground, and after you have done everything, to stand.
> Stand firm then, with the belt of truth buckled around your
> waist, with the breastplate of righteousness in place, and with
> your feet fitted with the readiness that comes from the gospel
> of peace. In addition to all this, take up the shield of faith, with
> which you can extinguish all the flaming arrows of the evil one.
> Take the helmet of salvation and the sword of the Spirit, which
> is the word of God. And pray in the Spirit on all occasions with
> all kinds of prayers and requests. With this in mind, be alert
> and always keep on praying for all the Lord's people.**

In light of this truth, every believer needs to put on the following spiritual armor each day:

- **Truth** (verse 14, our belt, which holds up the other pieces of armor)
- **Righteousness** (verse 14, breastplate which guards our body)
- **Peace** (verse 15, our shoes which allow us to walk in the Spirit)
- **Faith** (verse 16, our shield which guards us from darts of the enemy)
- **Mind of Christ/Thoughts of Salvation** (verse 17, our helmet which protects our minds)
- **Word of God** (verse 17, the sword which is our weapon)
- **Pray in the Spirit** (verse 18, our communication with God)

Commissioned

If you are a believer, God has given you a ministry—be it in your home, at church, work, in the neighborhood, your child's school, or cross-culturally as a missionary or overseas worker. Every believer has been charged with the ministry of reconciliation, meaning reconciling others to Christ (2 Corin. 5:11-21). When you decide to serve God in any capacity, you will become a target for the enemy and a threat to the kingdom of darkness. Given this fact, it is important that we stay close to God and learn to usher in his presence on our own without the help of a pastor, preacher, ministry, or prayer partner. We need to know how to communicate and be filled by God. We also need to be aware of the spiritual attacks of the enemy and know how to both prepare and fight back. While in Africa, I learned to value my alone time with God and the ability to get in his presence for a fill up. I've seen the effects of not putting on my spiritual armor or choosing to spend time with neighbors, walk to the nearby market, or surf social media rather than praying or spending time with God. Satan looks for opportunities to attack believers who are tired, have not prayed, studied the Word, and put on their armor. I cannot stress this enough. I became very aware of the sneaky attacks of the enemy while I was serving or preparing to serve God more than in any other time in my life. I'm praying for your strength and that even when you do not have a prayer partner, you will stand in agreement with the prayers that Jesus has already prayed for you (see John 17) to become filled with the presence, love, and fellowship of the Father.

Spiritual Warfare Journal Prompt:

Think back on a previous major spiritual attack that you encountered. What was happening in your life at the time? What was the enemy trying to stop you from doing? What happened as a result of your response in the battle? Write these reflections down so that you can become more aware of the enemy's strategy and how he wages war on your specific purpose. Living life on mission or as a missionary is not easy. When you entrusted your soul to Christ, you became Satan's enemy. We have to recognize this and refuse to allow the dark moments and thoughts to get the best of us during our lives on mission.

Notes from the Field

This morning I was reading 1 Timothy 2 and a companion study guide. Verses 5-7 talks about how Jesus gave Himself. . . the study guide states, "You can give your time without giving yourself. You can give your money without giving yourself. You can give your opinion without giving yourself. You can even give your life without giving yourself. Jesus wants us to give ourselves just as He gave Himself."

Lord, how do I do that? How do I give myself?

September 14, 2019
10:12 a.m.

Notes from the Field

Today was a better day. . . visits, lunch with the neighbor, met new people when I went on a voyage for bananas, read bedtime stories to kids, and helped clean someone's dining room just because, attempted to evangelize someone who was already a Christian, kicked a soccer ball with my students and new friends, and I worked on 2 book projects. I don't feel tired and I don't feel drained. . . . I even learned more Swahili today. . .

I'm adjusting . . .

September 14, 2019
evening

PART 2

cultural immersion

Mission-centered cultural immersion takes dying to yourself for the sake of experiencing God's heart for the new place that he's placed you. It's a slow and painful death that leads to new life in the end.

- NATASHA T. BROWN

CHAPTER 8
slow cooking

"The Lord is not slow to fulfill his promise as some count slowness, but is patient toward you, not wishing that any should perish, but that all should reach repentance."

2 Peter 3:9

God is so patient with us. Patience is a fruit of the spirit that we receive as a result of our fellowship with Christ. It's also something I attempted to master in Bulima early on.

One day in October, Mama Nangale and I had planned an entire afternoon and evening for her to teach me how to cook on firewood. I arrived at her house shortly after 2 p.m. on Friday, October 25, 2019, which I thought was extremely early to begin dinner preparations. We started by lighting firewood on top of three rocks in the back of her house and placed a large pot of water on top. As we waited for the firewood to turn into charcoal, we went into the chicken coop to catch that evening's dinner. The chicken coop is on the side of her house, and it always offered quite a lively time whenever we entered. During the daytime, you can spot a rooster chasing a hen, pinning her down, and quickly engaging in intercourse. Sometimes, it seems as if they are embarrassed to see people watching them, and the female escapes and the chasing begins all over again. At dusk, if you walk past the Nangale household, you'll see Mama or *Mwalimu* ("teacher," her husband) Nangale ordering the ducks to get in line so that they can go back into their brick house behind the Nangale family home. There are close to thirty chickens, roosters, ducks, and baby chicks in this coop. I smile remembering the evenings when I called myself trying to help put the chickens up for the night, only to cause more commotion.

Dinner Preparations

Once we caught the chicken that would become our dinner, Mama Nangale led me to the opposite side of the house, gave me a knife, and instructed me to slice the chicken's neck to chop off his head so we could continue with our dinner preparations. After sawing at his neck twice, I knew that I couldn't do it. The chick looked like it was in so much pain, and my arms wouldn't let me apply enough force to cut off its head, so Mama Nangale took over. She put the chicken on the ground, put one foot on its legs and the other on its wings, and chopped off his head. The chicken squirmed around a bit until the final traces of life were gone, then Mama Nangale and I walked (with the chicken head and body in hand) closer to the house. She put the poultry corpse into a bowl, fetched the boiling pot of water that had been brewing on the rocks, poured the steaming hot water on top of the chicken's body, and instructed me to remove its feathers.

The process of defeathering the rooster, cleaning its body, burning off remaining feathers, making rice and ugali, cutting vegetables and fruit, and preparing the remaining touches for dinner took about seven hours. By the time the family and I sat down to eat, it was close to 9 p.m. Granted, this process was drawn out because of all of my questions, interruptions, and mess-ups during this lesson. When it was all over, I asked Mama Nangale if she'd rather cook on firewood or a stove, and she said firewood. Although the process was slow and arduous, she preferred the slower cooking.

That afternoon, her eldest son Musa taught me how to clean rice. When I heard about this process of sifting to remove sand, washing, and repeating that process, I initially thought it was all a waste of time. I was used to buying boxes and bags of white rice and never even considered what happened to rice prior to me picking it up from the grocery store shelf. The process of harvesting rice is cumbersome from an American perspective. Before the rice can be planted, the ground must be tilled and level. You prepare the seeds first by planting them closely together in muddy or moist/watery areas until they reach a certain height. Then, these small rice plants are uprooted and planted with more spacing between each for a few months. Seeds have to be planted in good soil, and it can take up to five months for the harvest to be ready. Now, this is when the process gets complicated. My Tanzanian neighbor described the harvesting process like this: the rice itself begins to turn brown as an indication that it is ready. It's then harvested by being cut in sheaves. After that, the sheaves can be threshed by banging them down on a hard surface or by hitting them with something like a stick until a good chunk of the rice grains fall off.

After all the rice grains are collected in their covers (hulls or husk), they can be stored until one is ready to turn it into rice you can eat. Before removing the husk, the rice has to be laid out in the sun for as little as a day so that it dries. This makes it easier for the husk to come off without breaking the rice. Since the sun actually heats it up, once the rice is dried, you need to allow it to cool off before taking it to the mill to remove the husk. The drying and removing of this layer can all be done in a day. Sometimes, people remove the husk by hand instead of taking it to the mill. Every time I hear the rice harvesting process explained, I grow exhausted trying to follow it all!

I asked one of the Nangales to explain the difference between the type of rice harvested locally, versus rice purchased from a store. Initially, I was told that the rice from the store is already clean. Some call it "good rice." However, that evening when we cooked both the rice that I had purchased from the store and the locally-grown rice that Mama Nangale already had in her house, we noticed the store-bought rice cooked faster on the gas stove we were using, leaving the bottom layer burnt. Additionally, the locally-grown rice that Musa had cleaned was fluffier and thicker, which for me tasted and felt much better. I would define the locally-harvested, fluffier option as "good rice."

I learned this important lesson over and over as a missionary. Although Tanzanian processes such as cooking, boiling rice, washing clothes, and even baking chocolate chip cookies take longer and consist of manual processes devoid of electronic luxuries like microwaves, stoves, and washer-dryer machines, the final results (at least for food) were just as good and often much better. In Tanzania, I learned to bake chocolate chip cookies, dinner rolls (which my neighbors call scones), and banana bread from scratch. I learned how to cook on firewood, and make food that we grew in the garden in my yard taste just as good as what could be purchased from a restaurant. That evening, I could taste a hint of smoke in the chicken dinner I had with the Nangales. This authentic goodness came from the firewood and charcoal preparation process. It was savory and delicious, and I imagine that if Mama Nangale lived in the States, we could find her operating a country, soul food restaurant someplace in the deep south of Louisiana.

The results received from the time it takes to let things marinate and soak in the flavor of its natural environment is not only applicable for food. This same principle can be applied for many of our day-to-day processes. Most of us from the Western world are more accustomed to getting things quickly. For my generation and younger, we prefer a microwave, not a slow cooker. However, just like good meals and homemade cookies, as vessels prepared for use by God we too are best after a process of slow cooking.

~

There are great promises in store for us when we wait for natural processes to run their course, just like it is when we know a delicious, hot homemade meal awaits us. God's Word tells us in Isaiah 40:31, "He who waits on the Lord shall renew their strength. They shall mount up with wings like eagles, they shall run and not grow faint." Renewed strength, soaring high, and running toward the finish line of our race are the outcomes of waiting patiently. When we wait patiently for God, the experiences we encounter on the way build our faith. The word that gets deposited in our soul reassures us that we too have a promise from God, which will show up any day now. While waiting on things to finish like food, laundry, and dessert, I sensed the Lord ministering to me, building my faith, and solidifying my inner core.

When I was a child, my family took a lot of road trips. We'd pile into our family van or the Nissan Pathfinder and drive from the suburbs just outside of Washington, D.C. to North Carolina, Ocean City, Maryland, Delaware, or even Kansas. I didn't appreciate those long journeys through valleys and over bridges back then, because my mind was focused on arriving at our destination. "Are we there yet? Are we there yet? How much longer," my siblings and I would ask. Today, many of us are still like impatient children when it comes to God's promises. While immersing in this culture, in the absence of excess, I learned the virtue of patience. Today, I want to encourage you not to be so quick to arrive at a destination that you miss the journey and what God is teaching you during the process of slow cooking

Patience Journal Prompt:

Are you in a slow cooking process right now? What could be the benefits of patiently waiting? (Hint: Imagine God's best for your life.)

Notes from the Field

I arrived in class to find that my students were not prepared. As a result, I was also unsure of how to teach today's lesson (although, thanks to Holy Spirit, it eventually worked out).

To top things off, after that, I received a long Facebook note from a Jehovah's Witness making the case against women preachers and Bible teachers, suggesting that I think it's ok for women to "lord over" men.

Lord, can you reveal anything you want me to know? Is it your will for women to preach and teach? I believe it is because you wouldn't have called or anointed us with your Spirit if it weren't!

October 29, 2019

CHAPTER 9

Holy Spirit university and class notes

**"Trust in the Lord with all your heart
and lean not on your own understanding; in all your ways submit to him, and he will make your paths straight."**

Proverbs 3:5-6

I remember how quickly I rushed to my graduate university library and searched the catalogue for the most appropriate books with which I could teach. That warm August afternoon, about three weeks before leaving for Tanzania, I checked out close to fifteen books, went home, and dived in, desperately searching for which textbooks would be most appropriate for my theological studies and English courses. I had just learned that the syllabi were not exactly complete or robust enough to prepare me for twelve weeks of teaching, and students did not own textbooks for their courses. I hadn't expected to develop my courses from scratch and choose my own textbooks. This was a new challenge into which I dived head first.

In place of their own textbooks, students relied on class notes prepared by the teachers. Depending on the teacher, the notes could be just two pages for a twelve-week course or two dozen pages. I created my own class notes for three of my courses that term, but thankfully another longtime instructor gave me notes for the Christology course I was teaching. I would bring the books to class and my students and I would discuss points from the class notes. I'd stop us and read sections from the book, draw diagrams, or write definitions on the white dry erase board, and allow the students to collaborate for group projects and discussions. I didn't have access to projector screens, only handouts, the board, a Bible, and one book for me to lead our classes.

During my second term I taught three courses, and I didn't have any notes from other instructors. Instead, I prayed for guidance on how to prepare for our classes. I studied several books and my notes from seminary for hours each night or in the mornings before classes. I typed pages of notes for my students before our classes or photocopied pages from the books. I desperately wanted them to understand what was being taught, so my notes were extensive, with every major point from the textbooks. Sometimes, not feeling led to focus on the notes, I'd go into class unsure of how the Holy Spirit wanted to teach a specific lesson, but I'd simply surrender and open my mouth. A few months earlier, I had participated in the commencement ceremony for my master of divinity degree, and our chancellor said something I'll never forget, "Open your mouth and let the Lord fill it." I took this literally during my time as a Bible teacher.

It didn't take long for me to grow an appreciation for the preparation time before classes and the way the Holy Spirit showed up for our class discussions. I realized that just like my spiritual journey up until that point, the Lord was accelerating me (and this time my students) in the Spirit, and he was working through me to be able to teach effectively. Most importantly, he was teaching me to hear from the Holy Spirit as I stood before my classes. Before I entered the missions field, while in school for my master of divinity degree, I had been a ghostwriter for pastors, gospel artists, ministers, entrepreneurs, and PKs (pastor's kids). Listening to them talk about the Bible and then going to research topics on my own, all while studying theology in school, allowed me to take in a lot of information and gain deep spiritual knowledge fairly quickly. At the same time, a small close-knit church community, relationships, spiritual groups, prayer, prophetic meetings, and Christian fellowship helped me to grow in my personal spiritual life. It's so important for Bible students and teachers to have both theological knowledge coupled with true spiritual growth and discipleship.

During my first time as a missionary theological educator in Tanzania, I realized that I was in school with my students—together, we were in Holy Spirit University. But this time, he had me reading chapters of books each week before my classes, then going back through the chapters to type class notes. During class days, I'd walk my students through the notes, as the Holy Spirit led us in eye-opening conversations and observations. My students asked tons of questions, which allowed us to work through complicated concepts, such as Paul's argument in the book of Romans of how the Jewish rejection of Christ led to the Gentile opportunity to receive him, or the Apostle John's three marks for true believers and his definition of false teachers in the book of 1 John. The notes I prepared from theological books that had traveled in my suitcases from across the world and others, which I'd found hidden on the shelves of the Bible college library in Tanzania, surely had the wind of the Holy Spirit on them because those notes sparked much discussion and debate.

The lack of books and what (on the surface level) seemed like an inconvenience became a blessing for both me and my students. In the absence of excess, without enough books to go around for each student, we learned to search the Word and reconfirm what the theological experts were teaching us. Granted, this perspective could be solely my own. The idea of class notes is not a new concept to my students, but it was yet another opportunity for me to grow and experience this culture from within. Without having textbooks of their own to use outside of class it becomes necessary to understand the work during class, work together in student groups, and seek instructors for clarification. The students also spent a lot of time in the library and its computer lab. In both

Inductive Bible Study and Bible Interpretation classes, my students and I dove deep into the hermeneutical implications of various genres and books of the Bible. I *became* a theological teacher in practice, not just in title or theory. It was a great blessing. In addition to the experiences and discussions, recordings, and pictures from the class time I spent with my students, both them and I have dozens of pages of notes on various theological subjects so we can remain students and teachers of the Word. God never ceases to amaze me. He called me to be a teacher and taught me how to teach by teaching me what needed to be taught in the form of class notes and the wind of the Holy Spirit. It's easy to complain or panic when we don't have our usual "helps" or luxuries available, but these instances present opportunities for the Holy Spirit to show up as our teacher.

Holy Spirit University Reflection and Journal Questions:

Are you able to submit your intellect and agenda to the Lord to embrace what God wants to teach you? Could the Lord be desiring to teach you something outside of all the extra study material and online voices? What if you could hear God clearly and learn more in the absence of the excess voices or books about God? Is there an opportunity for you to submit your ear to the Holy Spirit?

Notes from the Field

I keep thinking about this prophecy I received from a friend on Sunday, August 25, the weekend before flying to Tanzania as a first-time missionary:

"Even as you teach these people it's not going to be teachings from your mind, it's going to be teachings from your spirit where he's going to release an impartation into their lives. I see that you're a mobilizer. You're going to mobilize them. Literally they are going to come into your classes at one level, not full of zeal and passion, but they're going to leave on fire. They're going to be fire starters in Africa. You're going to hear testimonies of 'Oh that student did this!'. . . You called out their destiny and their potential and they're going to walk in it. You're going to impart confidence and boldness into them. These men are going to figure out how to be real men in their valor and walk into the destiny and capacity that God has called them to. You're going to also be imparting lots of knowledge and joy and love into the women and children . . . The Lord is giving you authority over that oppression . . . You're going to lift these captives from oppression and they can walk in authority and they don't have to be submerged.

It's not going to be just a syllabus that you'll be following, but it will be the Holy Spirit. You'll walk in a class with a plan and the Holy Spirit will take over . . . I see creativity. No class is going to be the same. It's all going to be so unique, and people are going to walk out like *whoa what hit me . . ."*

CHAPTER 10
Holy Spirit, come

There are many Christian cultures around the world that do not believe in the spiritual gifts and offices, often referred to as the five-fold ministry. There are also many Christian cultures that are not educated in the baptism of the Holy Spirit and whose theology do not include the gifts of the spirit. I grew up in the black Baptist church and cannot remember any talk of the Holy Spirit, spiritual gifts, apostles, or prophets so I do not want to assert that those who do not teach about spiritual gifts and the Holy Spirit are not true Christians. Many are, but there are also false religions and denominations that deny the third person of the Godhead which is the Holy Spirit. In this chapter, I am speaking of genuine Christians who had not been taught or had not embraced the spiritual gifts and manifestations of the Holy Spirit. I learned there was a lack of demonstrative power and a level of oppression because of this.

In my own life, It was not until I grew older into my late twenties or early thirties that I was introduced to the fullness of God in terms of his power and the workings of that power today through the Holy Spirit and spiritual gifts. It was then that I was also awakened to my own spiritual gifts and calling as a prophetic evangelist and teacher of the Word. I grew a hunger for the Word and deep treasures of God in my early thirties after God delivered me from a toxic relationship. This awakening signified the end of one chapter—and life in a sense—and the beginning of a new life in Christ. During the beginning days of my new life, I sought God more than ever before because my desire was to learn more about him and to become like Christ. I wanted to understand who God is and awaken to my identity in him. I started to search for and attend classes at local churches. I came across a few that blessed me including a Spiritual Gifts and Callings course. I learned about the gifts of the spirit. I learned about and interacted with apostles, prophets, evangelists, and teachers and started to understand their roles and purpose in the body of Christ. I began to desire the gifts, and I realized that certain gifts had always been inside of me. Needless to say, during this new season of my life I sought God with every part of my being. I was delivered from many fleshly desires. I also learned about the church structure and apostolic ministry.

Fast forward: I didn't know what to expect when I went to the mission field in East Africa, but the week before my departure the Lord began to speak to me about the spirits of legalism and religion in order to war against them in prayer. These are clear enemies to the gospel as we see in the New Testament accounts of the evangelists. The people who opposed Jesus' miraculous ministry and his mandate to heal, save, and deliver (by any means necessary) were those who were so high and mighty with religion that they failed to connect with the people and embrace the work of the Messiah. These same religious types persecuted Paul and the apostles in the book of Acts. Those bound by the spirit of religion embraced the law instead and missed the Messiah. They turned a blind eye to the miracles, killed Christ, and attempted to silence his name. The nation of Israel and Jewish people have since been blinded, in large part, to the ministry of Jesus. Religion and legalism leads to spiritual pride which puts a clear barrier to discipleship. Sin, of any kind, leads to death. Legalism and the religious spirit lead to murder, and as the New Testament shows us, denying Christ's power is demonic and dangerous.

~

I arrived at my mission post and was immediately moved by the deep passion that most of the Christians had for God, their relentless pursuit of the gospel, and how the ministers in training were extremely committed to sharing the gospel to unreached people groups. I was blown away by their level of reverence for God, commitment to holiness, and right living. I admired their family devotions after dinner time, their willingness to give up their lives to follow Jesus, and their devotion to saving lost souls. Furthermore, their worship style of Swahili praise, dancing, and corporate prayers made my heart smile. I've already mentioned how willing the believers are to pray and tarry for those in need, which was all very sweet to my soul. I was impressed and I almost snoozed on the warnings I had received from the Holy Spirit about some issues that were also present and working against the gospel and the move of the Spirit.

During my first term in Tanzania, I taught four courses. Two of them were Inductive Bible Study and Personal Spiritual Development. I thought for sure that these courses would allow the Holy Spirit to teach as he wanted on the matters of the Spirit—which they did. Our classes were filled with revelation and spiritual downloads just as my prophetess friend had foretold. My time teaching within classes and talking with students made me realize, in part, why God had warned me about the religious spirit. It also made me realize more reasons why I was called to that small village in a remote part of Tanzania, 7,000 miles away from home. Nobody spoke in tongues in public. In fact, this gift was looked down upon by most. Church meetings were filled with so much dancing and preaching, but no spontaneous moves of the Spirit. No hands were raised in complete surrender to the Spirit and nobody laid hands for healing. Yes, what I am describing probably sounds charismatic. I know not all churches in the West are like this either. I had been sheltered from the Holy Spirit's power and role within the Trinity well into my adult life. I had to build up my faith and get around believers who embodied faith and embraced the supernatural to fully understand and believe the Word of God in its entirety. I'm talking about the move of the Holy Spirit and his ability to empower us to receive and minister healing, work miracles, and witness the true power of the cross.

In Luke 9:1, Jesus gave his disciples the power and authority to drive out all demons and to cure diseases. In Acts 1:8, he told them that they would receive power when the Holy Spirit came upon them. Now that Christ no longer walks this earth as he did with his disciples, this *dunamis* (dynamic) power is only available to believers by way of the Holy Spirit. I realized why God sent me there. Many of my beloved students' eyes had been blinded just like mine in the past because of false teaching or teachers who did not understand, and therefore did not teach the true word of God as it relates to the Holy Spirit and spiritual gifts. Furthermore, their traditions, just like the one I had grown up in, had not included spontaneous worship, hands raised in surrender to God, speaking in tongues, prophetic utterances, and visible miracles.

During my Inductive Bible Study class, when we came across passages like Acts 2 about the Day of Pentecost when believers in the upper room received the Holy Spirit and the gift of speaking and understanding diverse tongues; or 1 Corinthians 12, when the Apostle Paul discussed the spiritual gifts, without fail, a student (or several) would raise their hands and share a teaching that they had heard in their churches where a leader had taught that these gifts were no longer active or relevant. I learned that the students were taught to ignore or worse, misinterpret, clear examples of the spiritual gifts at work. I learned that much of their resistance to spiritual gifts came from the early Christian influences from missionaries who brought Christianity (mixed with traditional, Anglican, Catholic, and other influences) to Tanzania and also the honest desire of believers in these villages to keep their Christianity pure from the mix of African traditional religions and witchcraft. So-called prophets and witch doctors often sounded the same to the Christians here as those from charismatic movements, which made so many shy away from the supernatural manifestations of spiritual gifts. I learned that Christians here often denied the validity of prophets because those who had claimed to be prophets were actually proven to be false prophets. Many of the students had also been taught not to question authority, desire spiritual gifts, or receive prophecies. I remember the times after those classes when I could feel that the Holy Spirit living inside of me was grieved. Yet, I knew the Spirit did not want me to stop speaking and teaching the truth. My assignment became more clear to me.

Once I was teaching about prayer and I shared some passages from the Bible, other spiritual life books, and my own experience with receiving my heavenly language, the gift of speaking in tongues (from 1 Corinthians 12:10). One student was so upset and he may have determined in that moment that I was a false teacher. He said, "No, I don't believe that" as he shook his head in disagreement with me. Immediately, some of his classmates spoke up and said that they too had previously believed what their leaders taught until they sought the Lord and learned about the spiritual gifts for themselves. Unbeknownst to me, two of my students had received their heavenly language before, and others desired the gift. One month into this mission, I felt a heavy burden from the Lord to continue teaching about the Holy Spirit both in my classes with small groups of students and corporately when I had an opportunity to minister at chapel services, nearby schools, or churches.

My Personal Spiritual Development class focused on the spiritual disciplines to help students grow deeper relationships with God and yield to the Spirit's working in their lives. This class provided me the opportunity to teach about prayer, praying in the Holy Spirit, soaking prayer, personal spiritual retreats, and other spiritual practices and disciplines. It was a blessing to see the students' transformation and especially to read their final essays, which all expressed their growth and deeper understanding of spiritual matters. I knew God had planted me right where he wanted me so he could usher in the kingdom within the next generation of Tanzanian ministry leaders. As I sensed what God was doing within the hearts, minds, and spiritual lives of my students through our classes, I was constantly reminded of yet another prophecy I had received on April 26, 2019 by a prophet in Virginia Beach who shared God's heart about my calling. Here is some of that prophecy that continued to come to my mind while I served in Tanzania:

"It's very apostolic what [God] has you doing, moving from place to place quickly, setting up, and bringing the kingdom of heaven in."

I know in order for believers to operate on heaven's agenda, we must be willing vessels for the Holy Spirit to work through. The ministers I've been called to in Tanzania are going to unreached people groups to reclaim territory for God. They are literally the laborers that Jesus told us to pray for to go into the plentiful harvest in Matthew 9:38. They need the full power of the Holy Spirit.

By the time October hit, I was very clear about my assignment. I was to continue ministering about the ministry of the Holy Spirit and to help the students share their stories. Although I had gone to Tanzania under the auspices of a theological educator and I taught a set of classes, I felt like I was on a covert mission for Jesus. God wanted to break the students' dependency on learning strictly from their church leaders and wanted to lead them into gleaning wisdom and knowledge from him through our helper Holy Spirit. In November, one of my phenomenal students, who appreciated my teachings on the Holy Spirit and the supernatural asked me to minister at a workshop in the local church. The workshop topic was the "Power of the Holy Spirit." After I ministered on this subject, a woman raised her hand and asked what I thought about the gift of speaking in tongues. I shared my beliefs that it was one of the gifts of the Spirit that Christ gave to church (Acts 1:8, 2). I told her that it is for all believers and we should have faith to receive the gift. I told her that this gift edifies us and helps strengthen our faith as well as allows us to pray in the Spirit when we don't have words (Rom. 8:26); it also gives us a way to worship God intimately and personally. She then asked me why so many of their leaders in the church teach contrary to what I was saying and what I had shown her in the New Testament. I explained to her that often people believe what they are told and taught, especially when it comes from people they trust. God himself can show and tell people something contrary to what leaders tell them and they will believe the voices of human beings over God. Regarding this spiritual gift, Liardon writes in his book *God's Generals*:

> "The Word tells us that 'praying in the spirit,' or in tongues, enables us to pray the perfect will of God into every situation because praying in tongues moves us into the realm of the Spirit . . . There are several different operations of tongues spoken of in the Bible . . .(see Acts 2:8-11, 1 Corinthians 1427-28; 2 Corinthians 14:4; Jude 20; Romans 8:26-27; Ephesians 6:18). If you haven't experienced the baptism of the Holy Spirit with the evidence of other tongues, then earnestly seek God for this. Speaking in other tongues is not just "for some." It is for everyone, just like salvation."[15]

As time went on, I continued to labor in prayer and in the classroom for my students to seek discernment and understanding from the Spirit about the matters of God. I wanted to teach them to fish for the truth for themselves, to truly seek God personally, not just corporately. I also learned that in this particular denomination people are used to corporate prayers, services, and chapels, and the other parts of their lives are so full with cultivating or working, cooking, manually washing clothes and taking care of their homes, which are often filled with extended family as well. Their lives are so busy and they have so much pressure on them that they don't always have time for things like personal spiritual retreats, hours-long prayers, or sitting with God in deep study by themselves. I don't want to stereotype or generalize, but I want to note that one of the results of living in a society such as

---

15. Roberts Liardon, God's Generals: Why They Succeeded and Why Some Failed hardcover reprint edition, (New Kensington: Whitaker House, 1996), 121.

the village, in the absence of excess, is that it's a different kind of busy or "excess" for that matter. There is so much work to do, so many visitors, and unexpected interruptions, that personal spiritual reflection can take a hit. I want to say this plainly, the village is *very busy*.

As my eyes were opened, I realized a benefit of our fast-paced, high-tech lifestyles—that often lack closeness—is that our excess speeds things up for us. Our fast internet makes it easier to do work and find information. Our washing machines cut out hours every week of manually washing clothes. Dishwashers and microwaves save us time. The cars we drive to work or church enable us to spend more time in church or work versus walking there. But perhaps, one of the greatest appreciations that life in the Western world gives us is that when it is necessary to turn off the distractions, the noise, and tune out the people, we have that choice. I can sit with the Word of God and allow the Spirit to speak to me. If I had a full-time job where I worked for another person or company, I could take a personal day to pray and fast if I needed to because my livelihood does not depend on one day of work or pay. I can forego corporate worship at church and not be judged negatively if I stay at home to seek God for myself. In Tanzania, some of these pleasures are just not realistic, and in the village, I saw a different kind of busyness and crowdedness. Even in my own life on Sundays in the village, I often had to close my doors and windows and put on my earplugs just to have quiet time with God for several hours. If not, visitors, loud music from the church, neighbors talking and laughing, and children desiring to come and sit with me would all prevent the quiet time I needed. While there is nothing wrong with any of these things, I realize that the type of personality and mind that I have requires lots of time alone with God. This was a constant source of torment because as a missionary you are always "on," and in the village interruptions are a regular. I had to fight for balance and time to be refilled by the Holy Spirit.

I want to be sure I paint a good picture for you—not slanted for or against the Christian traditions here. The continent of Africa is different from any place on earth. As a Westerner, I cannot nor did not want to force my way of life and thinking on my students and fellow believers. I completely respect the rich traditions and ways in which my neighbors in the village live out their faith. My desire for my students was for them to know God for themselves (not just from preachers and bishops) and not just God the Father or God the Son, but God the Holy Spirit, also, because Holy Spirit is truly our helper and the one person of God who still works in this world today to help believers walk in truth, power, and victory. It broke my heart that the Spirit was quenched here in terms of the spiritual gifts and five-fold roles of spiritual leaders, so even to this day, my prayer is still, "Holy Spirit, come."

Holy Spirit Journal and Prayer:

In the book of Acts of the Apostles, we see the Holy Spirit empowering the disciples and believers to minister, perform healing miracles, and boldly proclaim the gospel in the midst of persecution. The Spirit freed the apostles from prison and descended upon believers in the upper room which led to them receiving the gifts of diverse tongues and 3,000 believers being saved. **Do you believe that the Holy Spirit can move powerfully through you to empower you to witness about Jesus Christ through miracles? Be honest and dialogue with God on paper about your beliefs. Ask him to remove any limitations and barriers you've placed around the Holy Spirit. Pray for the Holy Spirit to come, infill you, and use you as a vessel.**

Notes from the Field

There's another side to the kingdom.

A side on the other side of the world - no smoke machines, bright lights, concert stages, huge bands, preaching shoes. There's a side that is much simpler - where people are warm, open, where there are endless lunches and dinners with neighbors.

Today was Pastor Lameck's welcoming day. He is the new leader of AIC Tanzania/Bulima. The church took an offering for him and his family during the five-hour church service. He preached a message about being faithful in our professions then led a communion service. After that, the pastor and his beautiful wife, Joyce, hosted the entire church and community for lunch and fellowship. Everyone (mostly men and four of us women) introduced ourselves. The other women were gathered outside, talking, cleaning, serving.

Of course I struggled with my Swahili, but my new neighbors were so gracious. All that matters is I tried.

There's another side to the kingdom of God where Christians live this thing [the Bible] out. Where the families eat together and share short devotions before meals. Where they aren't just seeking God for things, but the nourishment that never fades. There's another side of the kingdom, where people are inviting, where singing never ends, and everyone is always welcome home. Is this the side of the kingdom that I have been searching for?

Sunday, September 22, 2019
6:23 p.m.

CHAPTER 11

spontaneous surrender

"Iron sharpens iron, and one man sharpens another."

Proverbs 27:17

Often, the very area that feels deficient in our lives is the area where God wants us to sow. Pastor Steven Furtick of Elevation Church explained this point so poignantly in a sermon called "Needers and Feeders" rooted in Matthew 14, when Jesus led the disciples to feed the 5,000 men and children.

As evening approached, the disciples came to him and said, "This is a remote place, and it's already getting late. Send the crowds away, so they can go to the villages and buy themselves some food."
Jesus replied, "They do not need to go away. You give them something to eat."

Matthew 14:15-16

The disciples thought they were in need of food, but Jesus empowered the disciples to give an abundance of the one thing they thought they lacked, (food). Jesus not only met the crowd's need, but he also met the disciples' need to eat after they fed the 5,000. The disciples ate from the overflow (verse 20). The same is true in our lives. When we implement the principle of "sow where you want to go," we release what we have and make room for God to add more. Most importantly, we get out of our own heads and stop being consumed by our own needs so God can use us to meet the needs of others. I've applied this principle to my life at various points over the past five years and learned it to be a way to truly build my trust in God.

A disclaimer is needed, however. Despite my efforts to live by this principle, one day in mid-November during the time of intense attack, exhaustion and irritability hit me so strongly that I did not consider the spiritual realities of my situation. The concept of "sow where you want to go," was far from mind, and I simply wanted to sleep. I was tired.

It was a Sunday, after six days of working in the heat, teaching, English tutoring, and preparing four classes for final exams, I was exhausted and I felt depleted. I had already told myself that I would attend 8 a.m. English church service and go back home to rest and retreat *alone* until it was time to teach Bible study at 4 p.m. However, as I walked out of church, Abram, my missionary leader, asked me, "Hey Natasha, do you want to be spontaneous?" Although I knew my plans to sleep and rest, and the last thing I wanted to do was to be spontaneous if spontaneity required me to exert any energy, I surprised myself by answering, "Yes." I honestly think the Holy Spirit spoke through me because inside I was screaming as soon as that word left my mouth! He then told me we were going to hang out with his family in another village. Then, I learned that his wife, my friend on the mission field, would not be going, and it would be me, Abram, and his four boys taking the journey a few villages over to hang with his large Tanzanian family. Before we finally left an hour or so later, I attempted to take a quick nap, to no avail. I also attempted to think of any excuse to cancel and a reason why I couldn't go. No matter how many times I picked up the phone to cancel the plans I couldn't. The Holy Spirit would not let me back out. Sunday, the only day I could rest, was accounted for.

That day, God completely wrecked my plans to catch up on sleep and me time and decided to put me in the midst of a bunch of beautiful people instead. He once again showed me why, "It is not good for man to be alone," and why He calls us THE BODY of Christ. This day reminded me that God knows what we need better than we do. Had I remained at home, I would have gotten lost in my thoughts and allowed isolation to get the best of me. Or, I would have slept my day away and missed out on valuable fellowship. Instead, I participated in a spontaneous journey.

First we stopped in Nyashimo, a neighboring village that hosted the local market and bus stop to purchase mangos, bananas, ginger, and potatoes. Then, we drove about fifteen minutes down dirt roads to Shigala as I sat in the front of the truck videotaping the villages in between. Once at his family's home, a bunch of children and some adults surrounded the truck and took the fruit and vegetables from our hands to the back of the house where the mamas were already in the outdoor kitchen beginning to prepare lunch. Then, several of us adults along with a few children walked to a nearby English medium school because the family wanted to show Abram the newest developments to the construction project at the school, which is heavily supported by missionaries. I came back and visited a fabric store where I purchased a few pieces of kitenge, then I joined Loyce, Abram's sister in the "kitchen" located in the back yard of the house where her mother and uncle were already preparing lunch. In the kitchen, I mostly peeled mangos and cut bananas into small pieces while Loyce and I talked about many things, including what it's like to be an African American in Tanzania. As an aside, I found it sobering and soul enriching to share my feelings about this topic with her and to have her understand and confirm the reasons behind my feelings. You see, although I was embraced by the people I encountered on a daily basis, when I visited places outside of my village or even came across people who had never seen me in the village, I often felt like a science experiment. In addition to simply getting away and discovering amazing work being done between missionaries and people here, I received so much confirmation about some things God put on my heart. We took tons of silly photos, the eldest son showed me some of his video work, and, we ate a delicious meal. After dinner, we prepared to go back to our village. Before arriving home we stopped at Mary's house (a friend of mine as well as an amazing seamstress who works as the nanny for Abram's family). We stopped and visited with Mary and her son. I had so much energy when I finally returned to Bulima. I no longer felt depleted or like I needed a break from people. It had been a challenging couple of weeks, but this day was a testament of the Father's love for me. God certainly knows what we need better than we do. I wanted to be alone, but he knew I needed to connect with loving people who would connect me with his heart.

I am ever so thankful to Abram for the invitation to "be spontaneous." I was able to connect with people I had never met, and thoughts that I had in my mind were confirmed in the process. Proverbs 27:17 tells us that iron sharpens iron, just as one person sharpens another. While being alone is good sometimes, often our answers are found within community. Just as Jesus used what existed, two loaves and five fish, to feed over five thousand people who were hungry and in need of a meal, he does the same with us. He empowered the disciples to give what they felt they were lacking in order for everyone's needs to be met. On that Sunday afternoon, the Spirit led me to do the same thing. I didn't feel like I had time, energy, or tolerance to get to know people, be social, talk and spend quality time with others, but it turns out that in surrendering my time, I found the solution and remedy for what I needed.

Will you take God up on his invitation to be spontaneous, to surrender when you feel like you have nothing to give, and to venture into the unknown trusting that he has your answers?

Surrender Journal Prompt:

In what area are you holding back where God could be calling you to surrender? How can you let down your guards and give what you've been holding on to? How can you sow what you need, to go where you desire?

PART 3

cultural appreciation

It is our responsibility to help others appreciate the cultures we've been blessed to experience, even if our experiences were just for a short time. This is how we foster global citizenship.
- NATASHA T. BROWN

This section is important to us as readers, disciples of Christ, and global citizens. I am a big advocate of cultural immersion and not just visiting or taking from cultures, but truly experiencing them and contributing.

Only by living in Africa for an extended period of time were the eyes of my understanding opened to this way of life and my appreciation for it developed. I pray that through this section, your eyes will also be opened more to the similarities (not only the differences) of your own culture to this one and those to which you are called.

CHAPTER 12

faithful outreach and evangelism

> "The Spirit of the Lord is upon me, because he has anointed me to proclaim good news to the poor. He has sent me to proclaim liberty to the captives and recovering of sight to the blind, to set at liberty those who are oppressed, to proclaim the year of the Lord's favor."
>
> Luke 4:18-19 ESV

On Monday mornings at the Bible college, students and faculty meet for ministry groups. Each group finds space around campus, either in the grass under a tree, on the outdoor stage where graduations are held, inside the chapel, or on lawn chairs outside of the chapel, which is where my group met each week. There were about seven of us on average each week. As I spent more Mondays with my ministry group, I came to truly value and appreciate their purpose.

At the beginning of the academic term, each student at the school is assigned to a local ministry. Most of the students serve at local churches within the denomination. Some, however, are assigned to ministries or churches within other denominations. In my group, there was a mixture of both. The reason why I've grown to admire and appreciate these groups so much is because they are focused on evangelism and ensuring that the gospel is advanced. Each week, every student shares observations and updates from the ministry. Sometimes there are student needs mentioned such as the need for transportation because of the long journey they must travel by foot to reach their ministries on Sunday mornings by 8 a.m. (sometimes in the pouring rain). There are also occasional complaints such as ministry leaders at the local churches failing to provide food for the students after they serve for a good portion of the day. Then, there are observations such as church membership decreasing or people choosing to stay home from church to work in their shambas (which is a big no-no in this society). I love that these groups are not solely designed to discuss the students' own thoughts or needs, instead, they are centered around prayer and solutions for their ministries in order to reach people for Christ.

We learn important facts such as the great abundance of children who don't have adequate clothing or come to church without any shoes because their parents couldn't afford to buy them. We learn about recent storms that have blown the roof off of a local church or happenings such as the choir director who decided to go on strike due to offense in her heart caused by a situation with someone else in the church. During our Monday ministry groups, each student shares updates, including a recap of the preached messages. They share their observations about challenges that local ministries face. Then they discuss items that need to be addressed in prayer. After everything is out in the open, we pray for the churches and ministries, the students, and their ministry leaders. We pray strategically based on what the students have shared.

However, there is something else quite amazing about these groups of student-leaders. After the worship services are over on most Sundays, the student ministers and evangelists assigned to each church actually go from door-to-door to meet with people in each church's surrounding village. Their focus is to connect with people who have been absent from church or to offer pastoral counseling, prayer, and encouragement. They also aim to fill the local churches with those who have stopped attending or who have started to trust in witch doctors or false gods. Many of these house visits lead to individuals turning to Christ, returning to church, or at least committing to return the following week.

~

Google defines evangelism as *"the spreading of the Christian gospel by public preaching or personal witness"*. I like this definition because it gets at the heart of the purpose of our evangelism which is to spread the gospel in public or from person-to-person. This activity may or may not lead to conversions. In researching for a sermon series that I preached on evangelism, I discovered it can be directed at people who already confess Christ as their savior or those who don't. In the first case, often believers fall into a backslidden condition, or life circumstances sometimes lead our brothers and sisters into situations that seem hopeless. Many times what people need to hear to become and feel whole again is the good news of the gospel which confirms there is always hope with Christ on our side because of the promises provided through his life, death, and resurrection.

We often think about evangelism as the act of simply going out to preach the gospel to people who are unsaved, but truth is it's the simple act of proclaiming the gospel and making disciples. Everyone who has received Christ or I should say who has said the prayer of repentance (or salvation) has not become a Christ disciple or follower. There is so much brokenness within the global body of Christ. There is church hurt that goes unspoken, confusion due to wrong teaching, legalism that leads to condemnation which keeps people away from corporate fellowship. And in many churches love, the one factor that truly makes us disciples of Christ (John 13:34-35), is absent. When these issues exist, they can all be uncovered or discovered if we would simply take the lead from the formula set forth in the Bible and Monday ministry groups: reach OUT instead of waiting for people to come INTO the church. Believers should visit homes on a regular basis, not just when people are sick and shut in. This is easier to do when the four-walled church building is in a village setting as it is in Bulima. People travel mainly by foot or piki, with a few cars here and there. It's more challenging to visit people's houses after church when they live in a high-rise apartment building with keypad entry or gated communities such is the case in many North American communities. It's more challenging, but not impossible. Evangelism and outreach is an inconvenience for many Western churchgoers, given the desire to go out to brunch, get home in time for Sunday football, or complete assignments around the house on Sundays. Every community has their challenges. In East Africa, the challenges include finances, lack of vehicles and other socio-economic concerns. In America, our biggest challenge is often the excess that gets in the way of Jesus' command to make disciples and the way he showed us to do it—personally and individually.

I first wrote this chapter in February of 2020 while I was in Tanzania, prior to the world going on lockdown because of COVID-19 when church gatherings in America had not moved completely online. By mid-to-late 2020, it was a different reality, but I believe the Lord strategically sat the American church down and provided us with an opportunity to do church, evangelism, and discipleship differently. In many places, gatherings larger than ten to fifty people are prohibited. This leaves an opportunity to return to smaller gatherings, Internet worship, or even door-to-door evangelism that is quite prevalent in East African villages.

I remember when I first started in ministry. I began by facilitating small groups for women in a low-income, crime-ridden neighborhood in Washington, D.C. We had an amazing group of women who were all survivors (or working to become survivors) of abuse, drug addiction, or sexual assault. There was one lady who I adored with all of my heart who was struggling with an addiction to drugs. Some weeks she'd skip group, which made me concerned about her health and whereabouts. One week, when she skipped, I left our group and went to her house because I knew it meant she was probably either looking for drugs or coming down from a high in her apartment. She resisted when I showed up at her door, but eventually pulled herself together and reluctantly got into my passenger seat to join us at group. I had each member of the group set goals, which they shared, along with their progress toward those goals each week. For a month or more, week after week, the dear soul mentioned above would say she wanted to be able to return to her church, which was two blocks away. After a few weeks of hearing her empty wishes to return to church, I finally asked her, "Well why can't you just go to church?!" Crickets. "Okay, I'm coming to pick you up this Sunday morning and we are going to your church!" She was happy to accept my offer. I realized that sometimes people not only need a push, but a partner to join them in getting over the metaphorical mountains. That following Sunday, we returned to her church where she reconnected with a small group and the pastor she missed so dearly. It was so beautiful and I wished I could pick her up each Sunday to ensure she would keep it up. I lived forty-five minutes away from her and I also served on the social media ministry in my own church at the time, so I couldn't be there with her each week. However, that one Sunday made me feel like I was doing what Christ would have done: OUTREACH.

Something amazing happens when these ministers at the Bible college go out to do evangelism on Sundays—the walls come tumbling down. People are set free from oppression. They learn what is bothering neighbors in the villages. They come face-to-face with the unspoken evils tormenting their neighbors. Sometimes they just sit and offer themselves as a safe space and an ear to listen. They learn about what is happening in the church behind closed doors, and sometimes God miraculously provides for their own needs through people who they meet during these house visits. One Monday, our group leader for the week mentioned that the church leaders had not prepared a meal for the student ministers who are all struggling financially. But when they went out to do evangelism, they met a kind woman who was preparing food and she offered them a meal. How biblical is this? My heart warmed to know that even when we as so-called leaders miss the mark, God always has a way to provide for his children. The student ministers and local church evangelists leave their door-to-door outreach efforts with a prayer agenda and they show people a human side of the church. How much more would you be inclined to attend a ministry if you knew that the leaders cared enough about you to visit your home when you are absent from corporate fellowship?

Prior to going to Tanzania, I had spent nearly five years operating an online ministry and business. Many of the people we touched virtually through both organizations are people I have never met in person. In America, our society is so advanced that we have figured out ways to do church online via church platforms, Facebook Live, Instagram Live, and Periscope. We have online chat rooms and e-groups, discipleship programs delivered through email, and we "love" everyone without ever needing to meet them. Even when I served my former local megachurch as a member and trainer with our social media ministry several years ago, almost an entire year of my service on that ministry was done from the comfort of my own home because, at the time, I suffered with severe post-traumatic stress disorder (PTSD) and social anxiety and didn't feel healthy enough to be in a megachurch around thousands of people. I served faithfully online by watching broadcasts on my computer and using my phone to post tweets, Facebook, or Instagram content. In my native society, our advancements have led to a disconnection from people, and in some cases, a laziness to reach people through the gospel the old-fashioned way that we see in the New Testament which is up close and personal, on foot or door-to-door.

I was impressed by the simple concept of ministry groups at Nassa Theological College. Although inconvenienced, these students are faithful. They have a zeal for ministry and a passion for God and doing his work that is quite rare in some other parts of the world. They travel to churches by foot, which often takes them an hour or more each way. Those who are lucky enough to have transportation, like old-fashioned bicycles, borrow them from the school. The storage container where these bikes are kept is behind where I lived, and faithfully on Saturday mornings starting at 7:30 a.m., I heard clanging and clacking from that container. Some of the male students came to do maintenance on the bicycles in preparation for the next day's journeys. Evangelism is not going to always be, nor is it supposed to be, convenient. When Jesus gave us the Great Commission (see Matt. 28:18-20), he said to go into all the world. He didn't tell us to stop going when conditions were inconvenient. He didn't tell us to go to the church building and preach. He said go into the world. First, we should go into our worlds that are closest to us such as the communities nearby, the city where we live, our blocks, neighborhoods, and neighborhoods around our churches or schools.

When I lived in Virginia Beach, the small church I attended relaunched its evangelism group, and I was amazed with the number of people who gave their lives to Christ randomly on a Saturday morning. I remember stopping a young woman who had just parked her car and was walking into her friend's apartment building. She wasn't thinking about church or Jesus, but she had experienced a bad morning and the words of hope that me and my evangelism partner had shared with her let her know that "there is a God," as she proclaimed. She was happy to get her life right with Christ that morning. In Romans chapter one, the Apostle Paul says that he is not ashamed of the gospel because it is the power of God to save all those who believe. We too should take on this attitude and go and reach out without fear, laziness, complacency, or reservation. Ministry groups and evangelism is something done well at this Bible college in the rural inland of Tanzania and a case study for us in more, so-called advanced cultures.

Faithful Evangelism Reflection:

Jesus told us to "Go therefore and make disciples of all nations, baptizing them in the name of the Father and of the Son and of the Holy Spirit, teaching them to observe all that I have commanded you . . ."

(Matthew 28:19-20 ESV).

When was the last time you shared the life-saving gospel of Jesus Christ with someone? How can you add Christian outreach, evangelism, or discipleship efforts to your life?

Prayer:

Heavenly Father, we come to you in the name of Jesus first thanking you for exposing us to what faithful outreach and evangelism looks like. Lord, we ask that you open our hearts and minds to more opportunities to share your word, reach out to people around us with your truth, and discover the barriers that are keeping people from receiving you fully. Lord, we also pray that you will send more laborers into your local and global fields to bring your harvest of souls into the kingdom. In Jesus' name we pray, amen.

CHAPTER 13

industrious entrepreneurs and the tanzanian economy

"All hard work brings a profit, but mere talk leads only to poverty."

Proverbs 14:23

I t was a Wednesday afternoon in October, and I had just finished teaching a Christology course to seven pastors and evangelists. I caught a piki down the long dirt road to Nyashimo, a village about ten minutes away from Bulima by motorbike. When we arrived at the busy market area where the bus stop was located, a friend and I caught a crowded bus to Mwanza, which was a two hour ride. After spending a day visiting different shops, a bookstore, street stands, and eating at a local cafe, we headed to the bus station for our safari home. As we walked closer to the row of buses, several men approached us offering to help us find the right transportation and route for our journey. They were aggressive and I was following closely on the heels of my friend who is a native and had probably gone through this routine hundreds of times before. He ignored the overzealous helpers and I followed him to a bus in the front of the row of about five others, and we purchased our tickets. Once we were clear of the crowd and on our coach bus, he explained to me that the various men who had bombarded the travelers were all independent workers who received a commission for each traveler they brought to a bus line and who purchased a ticket. We found seats toward the front of the bus and I stared out of the window at the industrious men who worked these buses all day long. Knowing that this is how they fed their families made me wish I would have slowed down, talked to one of them, and allowed him to book my bus ride home, even if I would have paid a few dollars extra to do so.

That evening, it grew dark while we were on the bus and I remember stopping a few times at bus stops in villages along the way. When we pulled up to the first station for passengers to enter and exit, it was around dusk, yet the stop was full of activity. One mama walked up to my window. I vaguely remember her and the tan and brown kitenge cloth she wore which held her baby close to her chest. She had a bucket of roasted corn on her head. This young mama held a handful of slightly burned corn on the cob in her hand close enough for us passengers to reach out and grab them. The girl who sat next to me did just that. She asked me if I wanted a piece of corn in Swahili, and I shook my head no. She then paid the mama who stood outside, closed the window, bit off a few kernels from her corn on the cob, and placed them in the hand of her small son who was sitting on her lap. A few minutes later, she opened the window and waved down another food vendor outside. This next merchant was a woman selling chicken kabob strips wrapped in aluminum foil. The mother sitting next to me put her money pouch down in her bag, which was on the floor at her feet, and just like that she and her son began to enjoy their hearty dinner: corn and roasted chicken.

"... Almost half of the population lives on less than $1.90 per person per day, so there is a lot of work ahead to improve the living standards of all citizens."

—Bella Bird, World Bank Country Director for Tanzania, Zimbabwe, Zambia and Malawi[16]

16. "Modest Reduction in Poverty in Tanzania: More Can Be Done to Accelerate Pro-Poor Growth," The World Bank Press Release, December 11, 2019, https://www.worldbank.org/en/news/press-release/2019/12/11/

Tanzania is a big country, and I don't claim to know how things work all over, but in this part, the entrepreneurial spirit is high while unemployment rates teeter from nine to ten percent,[17] and the amount of income earned remains deficient to provide for the basic needs of most families. People sell all types of home-grown and cooked foods including local favorites such as mandazi, ugali, and maize (corn). You can also find coconuts, bananas, and mangos on many blocks in the city. My student, who is a missionary, passionate evangelist, and prayer warrior has a vision to train future Tanzanian missionaries. To support his family, save for this vision, and provide for his own school fees, he launched a mini enterprise selling local honey harvested on a bee farm in his home village. There's a market on Sundays near the Bible college where anyone can go and set up a table or a mat and sell their goods. Throughout the day, people who are in charge of the market walk around and collect payment for the day's space, which ranges from 200 to 1,000 shillings. This market is similar to the American concept of flea markets. At the markets and in any village, city, or town, people not only sell food, but they also sell pens and pencils, hair grease, soap, livestock, and African-print kitenge cloth. There are also seamstresses who can sew skirts, shirts, or dresses on-site. I've gone to the market a couple of times with Mama Nangale, who searches around for the best tomatoes, onions, or peppers. I've watched as the local farmers who raise sheep, cows, or goats slaughter them at the Sunday market, and sell raw animal meat. They skin sheep on site and sell the fur too. The idea of multiple streams of income is a way of life. Take Mama Nangale, for instance, who is the living flesh of a Proverbs 31 woman. She teaches women at the Bible college, teaches American missionaries like me Swahili, sells eggs, and sometimes kitenge cloth. She grows all types of vegetables, and preaches the Word. One day the doctor

---

modest-reduction-in-poverty-in-tanzania-more-can-be-done-to-accelerate-pro-poor-growth.

17. In the "Labour Market Information in Tanzania, 2018," the Statistician General of the National Bureau of Statistics in Dodoma, Tanzania reports the unemployment rate at 10.3 percent in 2014 and 9.7 percent in 2018.

at the local dispensary came to my house with beautiful hand-woven rugs that he and his wife had made. I purchased a new bath mat from them, and arranged for another personalized rug.

In our village, people often came to the front door to sell their chicken and duck eggs. At different times, two students attempted to sell me whole chickens that they had raised to earn 10,000 shillings for their children's medical treatment. Others walk around with bananas, and there are several women and men who sell fish in Bulima as well. The village sits at the coast of Lake Victoria, and so there are tons of fishermen. Most often, the people we purchased fish from were saleswomen who wait at the lake to fill the orders they received and who partner with the fishermen to sell their catch of the day.

The neighbors know how to market their business ventures too: door-to-door and word of mouth still works. They are persistent and will negotiate the prices at your door before they take "no" for an answer. I realized at one point that my fish lady was over charging me and my neighbor, and I decided to switch vendors on the testimony of a family I trusted who were already happy customers of a different fish provider.

In these villages, some young men drive pikis as motor-bike taxis. My favorite piki driver was Benjamin. I had his number saved and would call him when I got caught in the rain after a ministry assignment or needed to get home from Nyashimo after dark or when it was blazing hot. Others are paid to cultivate.

In Rock City Mall in Mwanza, there are young men who stand in the front of the mall selling photos. They offer to take your photo for a fee and print the Polaroids for you. It seems like anyone who is able has multiple sources of income, but of course, these income streams, as in anywhere around the world, are often contingent upon other factors such as the weather, good health, and the ability to invest in something that will help with their ventures (such as cattle, chicken, cameras, a piki, vegetable seeds, or sewing machines).

Most of my neighbors work regular jobs as school teachers, nannies, maids, or local businesspeople; many also plant and grow several types of crops, which become the main food source for their families. However, they have skills such as sewing, baking, or sales, which they also put to use to add additional revenue streams to their households. My neighbors use their hands and the gifts God has given them to survive and bless others. I've met the most talented hair braiders, bread bakers, and dressmakers in Tanzania. As an entrepreneur myself, I've desired to introduce their talent and awesomeness to people in the United States to help them make a higher profit.

We are able if we are enabled.

Despite the entrepreneurial mindset, there is a lack of economic sufficiency in the village and country, and often due to this, there are other thinking patterns stemming from years of corruption, poverty, and oppression that influence the behavior and economy for Tanzanians and many African nations.

For decades, individuals have relied heavily on support from sponsors and missionaries. In the title of this book, I noted that the author is a "Black American Missionary" because this indeed makes me different than most missionaries in the country. In Tanzania, missionaries have become synonymous with white people, and white people have become synonymous with money. Therefore, there are a lot of monetary expectations associated with missionaries in general. There was a slogan that states, "tunaweza tukiwezeshwa," which means, "we are able if we are enabled." In other words, for a long time there has been a mindset perpetuated that Tanzanians need the support of other nations to survive. Some nationals believed that only when there was help from others would they succeed. This might be true for many because of other contributing factors, such as the fact that very few students pass primary education to attend secondary school, and therefore have fewer opportunities for higher education resulting in fewer high-paying job opportunities, but on the other hand, this mindset has perpetuated a dependence on sponsors. Granted, colonialism designed it to be that way.

When I returned home from the missions field, I connected with a group of Tanzanians in America who were part of the church denomination in which I served in Africa. There is a diaspora group of Tanzanians in the States (and a few of us missionaries to Tanzania) who meet virtually on Sundays to pray for the country. I had a conversation with the group leaders, Drs. Fabian and Dainess Maganda, about the mindset towards money in Tanzania. They were more than happy to share their perspectives, so I am including a large part of our discussion to add additional voices to the viewpoints. Dr. Fabian is a hospital chaplain in Georgia and an adjunct professor at the University of Georgia, while Dr. Dainess is the director of the African Languages, Literature, and Culture department at the same university.

When Dr. Fabian Maganda was growing up in Tanzania, his father taught him the importance of working hard in order to accomplish his dreams.

> "'My son, you are going to secondary school, and I don't have enough money to pay for your tuition and expenses,'" Maganda recalled the conversation with this father. "'But thank God that he has blessed me with a large land. When you come home from school, come straight home and work on the farm.' He was teaching me to work hard, so I could earn my own money, and that would help me continue in school. I worked hard in the shambas, and we used to plant cotton and vegetables. I did that through secondary school to complete my education. We need to change our mindset. Our country [Tanzania] has a lot of resources. We need to use the resources that are available and that will help us. Do I agree with the slogan, 'we are able when we are enabled'? Yes, we might need some help here and there, but that should not be the only way. We have enough resources that will help us succeed in life. That slogan needs to be changed."[18]

To break the cycle of poverty, Maganda suggests nationals can shift their thinking from expecting others to help them to instead

---

18. Conversation with the Magandas on Sunday, August 9, 2020 via Zoom.

look for ways to generate income on their own. He noted that farming cannot remain the way it has been for decades. Tanzanians must use the education they've acquired to develop more sophisticated methods for farming, he said. Business and education are the two avenues that give Tanzanians a fighting chance in the global economy. As the economy grows in the country, the mindset also needs to change Maganda added. During my time in Tanzania, I noticed a few problematic issues with the education system, which contributes to the economic viability of its residents. Students are taught in Swahili up until they are in secondary school, and then education switches for their final years of school to English. The best schools seem to be those that start with teaching the English language during formative years. These schools have fees attached that are far too expensive for the average family, aside from sponsors and support.

Maganda pointed out another issue that has led to negative thinking about money, especially in

Christian communities. In the past, missionaries have been a part of the problem. Dr. Maganda notes that there was a notion introduced by missionaries that Christian ministers cannot be engaged in business. In fact, they were looked down upon and even condemned by many, especially in this denomination, when they desired to be involved in business. This was a constant area of discussion and counsel with my students who desired to serve God yet they did not want to be poverty-stricken while doing it. In essays from my English class, a few of my students expressed these sentiments, having seen their pastor-fathers and church elders struggle in ministry without being adequately supported by the local churches yet, ironically, also being deterred from working outside jobs. They've been taught that ministers who do so are not faithful to the work of God. So, they depend on sponsors and missionaries.

According to Maganda, early missionaries to Tanzania were contributors to this mindset. They would tell people in Tanzania to "pray to the Lord" to bring support for their missionary work, but they did not tell them that they also had to work for this support, therefore it perpetuated a mindset in many that ministers cannot work. International missionaries to Tanzania, meanwhile, had to visit a number of churches and build a network to raise support, but they were not teaching these same principles to those in the African church. In Tanzania, I spent a great deal of time explaining my call to business and ministry to my students. I attempted to share with them a mindset of leveraging business to build the kingdom of God. This is in fact the example that the Apostle Paul set forth in the New Testament. He was a tentmaker to support himself so that he would not be a burden to the church. Dr. Dainess Maganda continued:

> "From a personal experience, people think that we came to America and people were showering us with money. We are not those Africans who came here and had people give us money to go to school. Churches didn't support us. No! We cleaned bathrooms, cleaned yards, and worked in cafeterias. We don't have student loans. God can bless you using your hands. He is the same God that touches people to give money. He can touch people, but don't forget that he can use the work of your hands to bless you," Dr. Dainess Maganda said. "It's also important to budget. . . There is a different mindset that comes with money given to you versus that which you have earned. When someone gives you money, you manage it differently than when you earn it."

The Magandas agreed that when people pray, God gives the wisdom on how to acquire money. The Magandas have been in the States for close to two decades as educators and ministers. They have also established ministries in Tanzania.

"You pray so that God can give you ideas on how to earn money. Most of my people pray so that people can bring money to them. It's just a mindset. I have such a big problem in us having to ask the white people to donate, thinking that's the only way that God is able to do big things. He is able to use us to do big things," Dr. Dainess said.

In a nearby village, one Christian missionary and businessman from Canada mobilized a number of donors to raise funds to build a school. Another missionary drastically improved the conditions of a nearby mission that provided shelter and schooling to street children in the city. Realizing the great need that exists and the heart you grow for the beautiful people here, I imagine that most missionaries who come find it quite difficult to leave this soil without looking back. Contributing to the future success of Tanzanians remains a heart's desire for me and others I know. I was blessed to spend some time at a children's rescue center in the city and meet one of its biggest supporters from the States. I learned about programs he helped start and I spent time with the staff and the American philanthropist as they celebrated high test and student achievements. It's obvious that the support was making a difference. During my time in Tanzania, I was blessed to have a few days away from the village to explore and minister at different ministries, this one included. Seeing so much need, and the effect of the seeds sown here put a drive in me to make my business endeavors successful, simply so that I could bless others in a greater way. I watched and heard stories of missionaries building schools, purchasing property for schools, and sponsoring Tanzanians to attend school. Being in the company of big givers inspires you to become an even greater giver as well, but I learned there are healthy and unhealthy ways to give, and some giving often hurts the recipients.

So how can Tanzanians break out of poverty? Dr. Dainess Maganda suggests "starting with what you have." She warns against the thought that a lot of resources are required to start a business. She suggests starting by selling small items like peanuts, mandazi, and other edible products that can be cooked or created with one's hands. "At every level, there is a way you can make money," she said. It happens *pole pole* (slowly slowly). "We [the Magandas] preach this gospel that God can use us to build his kingdom, without having to depend on support." As I set forth at the top of the chapter, I met extremely creative and hard workers in Tanzania, but I also met those whose thought patterns reflected that which the Magandas described.

A Deeper Look into Global Factors Affecting the Economy

According to Opportunity International, an organization that aims to end extreme poverty by providing financial access and opportunities to people in poverty-stricken nations, 36 million people live below the poverty line, and one in three people in Tanzania are self-employed. Our Tanzanian neighbors are smart, creative, and determined. If they were in a Western society, these same people who live with the bare minimum on less than two dollars a day would likely be middle class or wealthy business people providing solutions for others who would gladly pay top dollar for their custom services. I remember getting my hair braided. It took my hairdresser nearly twelve hours and her fee was twenty-thousand Tanzanian shillings, which was about nine US dollars at the time. I paid her more than she charged and also paid for a student who was there to get her hair done. Some of the women were completely blown away when I told them that the hairdresser could easily charge people $150 or more in the States for this same hairstyle (about 350,000 Tanzanian shillings). Reading this again makes me mad. I've been so distraught on many days knowing that the great blessing and gifts that Tanzanian people possess are not yielding a fraction of what they would be worth in the Western world. The hands of Tanzanians are prosperous and anointed. Whether they sew, sow, braid, or cook, the wealth of talent and wisdom I encountered is enough to produce wealth in our country, but barely helps them get by in theirs, despite their many sources of income. The economy is different in Tanzania. There is a greater value on products, than services, and a higher demand on basic-need items such as food than luxuries such as hair-dos. Besides, many black women in Tanzania wear short haircuts as a part of their culture. The value placed on certain types of services and lack of value on others (such as hair) is yet another major difference in a country without much excess to spend on luxuries that many people in Western cultures consider necessities.

As I began to research the economic disparities between the continent of Africa and other areas of the world, I realized this is the result of several factors including intentional abuse from colonizers that traces back to slavery, international leaders who desired Africa's natural resources but did not care about its economic prosperity, poor decisions on the parts of African leaders, and even the mindsets of some nationals. Africa has been exploited by other parts of the world and those within its borders for far too long. Africa is a complex continent and many factors affect the economy. In the introduction to his 1982 release *The Africans,* David Lamb wrote:

> "For every corrupt and callous African president stashing millions of dollars in his Swiss bank account, There is an African teacher earning $60 a month, proud that his students are Africa's hope for tomorrow . . . [This is] the story of people who won their freedom on battlefields and at negotiating tables, only to discover that their white colonial masters had been replaced by black neocolonial leaders more concerned with personal power and wealth than national consensus and developments."

Thinking about these issues opens a can of worms and a Pandora's box. I cannot discuss entrepreneurship or the economy without confronting the sad fact that despite the industrial nature of Africans in countries like Tanzania, other global economies exploit the continent.

> Since its inception, the logic of international aid from the West has been to integrate African economies into a global capitalist system, which relies on Africa's resources for its own growth. The way aid is given has never fundamentally challenged a relationship that has evolved over centuries to the detriment of the majority of Africans. Exploitation of Africa's people and its resources has been going on for at least the past 500 years and, as Guyanese academic Walter Rodney pointed out in 1973, Africa helped to develop the West in the same proportion as the West helped to underdevelop [sic] Africa. That story remains as true today as in Rodney's time.[19]

---

19. Firoze Manji and Pablo Yanguas, "Should the West Stop Giving Aid to Africa?"

This perspective has been echoed by various journalists, researchers, and academics.

> In the era of colonization, peasant farmers did their jobs under the supervision of the colonial masters. Even on the peasant farmers' own soil, the land on which they labored to sustain themselves and their families, the colonial supervisors decided how much the peasant farmers earned and determined the quantity of food that accrued to them on accomplishment of their daily tasks. Even in time of harvest, the colonial masters determined the price of the goods from the owners of the land (Andreski, 26). This practice was only a rehash of what was to come several years after the colonial masters left Africa. This was a process of the satellisation of Africa, where every economic activity on African soil is directed towards the needs of Europe (Oguejiofor, 39).[20]

This paper continues on to state that developed nations control the economic realities in the world, which lead to negative outcomes for poor nations. As it notes, problems begin largely when developed nations cajole developing nations to sign up to rules that make sense and are meant for the prosperity of the already developed ones. One evident example that spans through history is the patenting of products and natural resources that emanate from African soil.[21] A quick search with the World Intellectual Property Organization yields telling statistics that support the research above. Of the ten-year span from 2009 to 2018, 2018 was the only year where the number of Tanzanian resident patent applications topped those of non-residents.[22] However, in 2018, there were eighteen Tanzanian patents granted to entities outside of Tanzania and just six in-resident patents granted. (See the charts below. from the World Intellectual Property Organization statistics database.)

New Internationalist, December 17, 2018, https://newint.org/features/2018/11/01/giving-aid-to-africa.

20. Isaiah Aduojo Negedu, "The African Predicament," Internet Encyclopedia of Philosophy (A Peer Reviewed Resource), Last assessed September 10, 2020, https://www.iep.utm.edu/afr-pred/#sh2a.

21. Ibid.

22. World Intellectual Property Organization Statistics Database

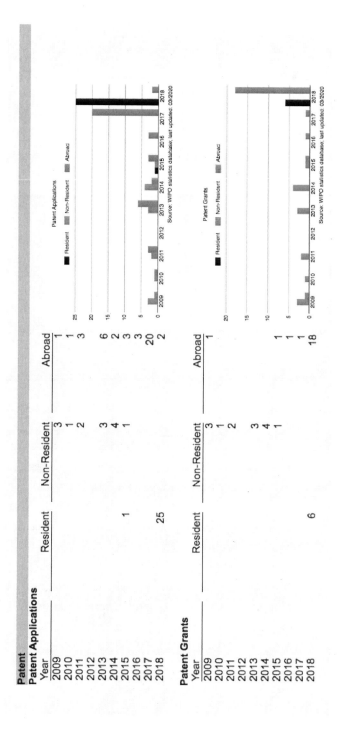

Patent
Patent Applications

Year	Resident	Non-Resident	Abroad
2009		3	1
2010		1	1
2011		2	3
2012			
2013		3	6
2014		4	2
2015	1	1	3
2016			3
2017			20
2018	25		2

Patent Grants

Year	Resident	Non-Resident	Abroad
2009		3	1
2010		1	
2011		2	
2012			
2013		3	
2014		4	
2015		1	1
2016			1
2017			1
2018	6		18

According to a paper entitled, "Scoping Studies on China-Africa Economic Relations: The Case of Tanzania"[23] released by the Economic Research Bureau in Dar es Salaam in 2008, after its independence in the 1960's Tanzania's policies became more radical, and they chose a socialist path for development for its domestic policies, yet on foreign policy, emphasis was placed on spearheading the liberation of other Southern African countries which were yet to gain their political independence.

> These developments exacerbated the growing hostility between Tanzania and the West and led to the need to secure new sources of external assistance. Thus, the socio-economic and political relations between Tanzania and other countries like China developed rapidly partly due to [Tanzania's first President Julius] Nyerere's desire to reduce the country's dependence on the West and to adopt a more non-aligned position in world affairs. It is precisely because of these changes in Tanzania's socio-economic policies, China became more willing to offer development aid (Bailey, 1975). This phenomenon also coincided with growth of the Cold War tensions between Moscow and Washington, where China remained independent and focused on other countries instead (Looy 2006).[24]

Today, Tanzania still depends on this relationship. I've heard some joke and call the country, "The Tanzanian Republic of China." Over the past several decades since the 1960s, there have been at least thirteen major milestones in the relationship between both countries with aid sent from China to Tanzania by way of human and tangible resources. By 2003, there were at least eighty Tanzanian students studying in China, and medical teams have been traveling to Tanzania from China since the 60s as well.[25] Tanzania is China's largest aid recipient. From military to medical support, technology, education, and import-export, China is interwoven in nearly every part of Tanzanian society. The

---

23. H.P.B. Moshi and J.M. Mtui, "Scoping Studies on China-Africa Economic Relations: The Case of Tanzania," Economic Research Bureau, Last assessed September 10, 2020, https://media.africaportal.org/documents/Tanzania-China.pdf.

24. Ibid.

25. Ibid.

questions remain, however such as who will benefit most from China's presence in Tanzania in the long-haul? Why is the poverty rate in Tanzania still so drastically high? These are rhetorical questions that cannot be thoroughly answered in such a short space, however, prayerfully from the various perspectives and research presented here, we have a better idea of the many factors that affect money in nations like Tanzania. Ultimately, this awareness of the deeply embedded factors affecting the economy and thought patterns should empower us to operate in grace, knowing that despite the money matters, all of us are made in the image of God. No amount of human exploitation, wealth, and even our personal views of ourselves because of what we possess can change that.

If Tanzanian history and the rest of the world are any indication, education and entrepreneurship in Tanzania will continue to provide opportunities for economic independence.

Prayer for the Financial Prosperity of Tanzania:

Dear Lord,

You've made us aware of some of the financial challenges facing the United Republic of Tanzania. Lord, we thank you for this awareness and for also giving us an opportunity to intercede for our neighbors in this beautiful country. Father, we ask that you would send God-fearing and honest leadership, Spirit-led missionaries and investors, and also finances into this nation that would provide opportunities for children and families to achieve financial independence. Lord, we thank you for the many gifts you have given your children. Please multiply the work of their hands. Raise up Christ disciples who will be your hands and feet to serve and give in Tanzania in ways that please you. We thank you Lord, in Jesus' name, amen.

CHAPTER 14
leave and cleave

"Therefore shall a man leave his father and his mother, and shall cleave unto his wife: and they shall be one flesh."

Genesis 2:24 KJV

Some of my best friends in the village are males. This is ironic given the unwritten cultural rules which assert that men and women should not spend time together alone. When people see two people of the opposite sex together, they jump to conclusions. One of my married missionary friends went walking with a student of the opposite sex and afterwards began to receive questions about their relationship status like, "Are you two married?" Even as adults in our thirties and forties, walking alone or talking intensely to someone of the opposite sex is a cultural faux pas.

When I first arrived in Bulima, I struggled with this cultural regulation. I wanted to explore and learn my surroundings. Most of my female students and faculty friends were married or busy. The weekends were the days when I found myself with extra time, but on Saturdays, most women worked in their shambas and on Sundays, the students all had ministry assignments and I co-taught a late afternoon Bible study.

It was the end of September, and I still hadn't seen Lake Victoria for myself. I decided that I would go to the lake, and my male friend agreed to walk with me. It was such a fun time. We walked thirty minutes right through the center of the village, sometimes finding dirt trails or following a young shepherd boy and several of his cows. During this trip, my friend, Musa, taught me about the dispensary, Simba Wa Yuda, a private school that teaches in English. We talked about cultivation and healthcare, and I learned about the process of building houses with mud and thick grass leaves. He taught me about rice pods and tomato plants. I saw mango and coconut trees up close and miles and miles of dry land where green vegetation would soon sprout. While walking to the lake, I learned about the water system in the village and the huge tank on top of the hill that supplies water to residents. I saw mud-like houses with grass roofs that do not have water or electricity. Mamas, who had just left the lake, walked uphill with buckets of water on their heads. We stopped by some students' homes who lived by the lake and were greeted by their chickens. Some of the female students were sitting under a tree reading their Bibles. When we finally reached the lake, fishermen were preparing to get into their boats and catch their food from Lake Victoria. Women bathed near the shore and my friend and I waited until they were done to approach the water. I took lots of videos and pictures of the scenery, and it remains one of the most special adventures of my time in Tanzania.

When we returned to our side of the village and I told someone about our trip, I was quickly reprimanded (for lack of a better term) about walking alone with a male. "Although you may not care, imagine how you could impact the people who see you. Once you lose their respect it will be hard to get it back," is what I was told.

At first I thought this cultural regulation was a ridiculous and archaic thing, but later I grew to appreciate the innocence of the culture. The village is extremely conservative and the believers attempt to live with the Bible as their standard. Whether I would deem it old-fashioned or not, there is a level of purity among the body of believers in this part of the world that can be a model for other cultures. Sex and disrespect are not a part of the conversations in the village, although I've heard it's different in other parts of the country. My male friends, who are unmarried, live at home with their parents. They help their parents tremendously by tending to the gardens, animals, work, and business when needed. Black men in their thirties still living at home with mom and dad is looked down upon in the United States, but here it is welcomed. While living in the village, my mind expanded and I was able to truly see how many cultures around the world build wealth for their families by sharing resources, including living spaces, business ventures, etc. It's smart and biblical to remain at home until marriage. Genesis 2:24 says, "a man shall leave his father and his mother, and shall cleave unto his wife." While the Bible does not make it clear whether or not there is a length of time between the "leaving" home and the "cleaving" in marriage, in American society we often think this leaving should happen long before one cleaves. Of course, our world often requires this due to people leaving home for college, job opportunities, or other responsibilities and personal desires. This happens in Tanzania as well. Some of my single Tanzanian friends left home for school or work, but they often returned to their parents and participated in building the home, farming, earning income, and working in partnership with their parents to ensure the continuity of the home. Something else happens before the cleaving as well. In Christian homes, I've seen the men expect and prepare for their wives. They are not out partying, sleeping with numerous women, or wasting valuable time. They are preparing, praying, learning, working, and serving their parents. Now, of course I'm speaking about believers of Jesus Christ, not those who live outside of God's covenant.

One of my male friends in his thirties, who lives with his parents, has begun making preparations for marriage. I didn't realize the magnitude of his preparations (and I probably still do not). He'd slowly tell me more of his plans as they came up in conversation. One day, I was sitting in his family's home and noticed there were two refrigerators, and his mom told me one was his. I later learned that he often spends the weekends in a village over an hour away because he's building a house for his future family. Each month, he takes some of his earnings to purchase bricks or other materials. By the time I left Tanzania in 2020, his house was fully constructed with just windows to add. He had begun making preparations for the day he will marry the wife that he had yet to meet.

As I thought about this one day, I realized the beauty and purity in it all. This lifestyle sets such a good foundation for families. It's not odd to hear that grown, unmarried men are virgins either. The sons realize their responsibilities to help their parents, especially if they are unmarried. The Lord illuminated for me the Scriptural relevance of these actions. Before I go on, let me just say that often one reason why unmarried children remain at home is because it's less expensive and helps the family economically, but it's deeper than money. It's also about the Word.

The Lord allowed me to see the purity in the family structure on various levels. I saw how, in the absence of excess, relationships are less complicated. There is a simplicity in choosing a spouse. I have listened to the testimonies of several "suddenly" marriage stories from the village. In some instances after attending school together for a few years, the man asked the woman if she would marry him, and seeing that they were compatible during in-class interactions, the woman said yes. These couples did not have romantic relationships prior to marriage. In other cases, couples were introduced by mutual friends, they met each other in person a couple of times, talked on the phone, and in a few months they were married. I've heard other testimonies where the man and woman were in the same place at the same time doing ministry together and a friendship grew. In every Tanzanian marriage story that I've heard (and I've asked a lot of people to share their stories with me), the common factor was that it was not complicated. In two instances, the only two that involved long courtships, one person broke it off after about a year into the courtship process. This isn't a scientific observation, but from my conversations, the simple pre-marriage processes have led to long, seemingly happy unions. These were all Christian marriages, mind you, so of course the ultimate factor which people communicated very clearly to me is that they spent most of their time praying about their spouses and the Lord confirmed it for them. After the initial attraction and interest, they simply relied on the Holy Spirit's leading to determine who their spouses would be. This is so sweet to me when I compared it to American tradition when people often take months and years to decide if they will marry someone.

The lesson here is that perhaps in American we make love and marriage too complicated. As a single person surrounded by many married people who loved each other with no strings attached, I was inspired by the stories of simple, "suddenly" love, but I have also been equally inspired by my friends who are still waiting to leave and cleave in a way that honors God and their families.

Leave and Cleave Reflection:

How would you feel if someone you were interested in romantically still lived with his or her parents well into their thirties? Do you believe your feelings about marriage and relationships are aligned with God's thoughts and God's Word?

Notes from the Field

Hanging with the mamas, celebrating the baby. I love the love that lives in this place. I'm serving with the Sukuma people of Tanzania. They are so warm and welcoming and are persistent about teaching me their tribal language.

February 9, 2020

CHAPTER 15

baby blessings

The village is full of babies and small children. I quickly grew accustomed to seeing women pull out a breast and feed their babies in the middle of chapel, at dinner or lunch, during comfort services, anytime their babies needed to be fed. During the first few months of my time in the village, one of my students in the diploma course asked our class to pray for his family because his wife was pregnant and they were hoping to have a baby girl in December. I met his wife, a cute, short and petite beauty with a short afro and warm smile at the school's opening welcome ceremony. She wore multiple pieces of kitenge cloth over her dress, and I would have never guessed she was pregnant. The following week, her husband Timothy came to me during a mid-morning break from our Monday English class and informed me that he and his wife would like to name their baby Natasha if they ended up having a girl. I didn't take this too seriously, but when the baby was born while I was home for the holidays, my student sent me a photo. Our prayers were answered. She was a healthy, chocolate cutie pie with chubby cheeks and beautiful brown eyes. She actually reminded me of the baby pictures I had seen of myself, and her name was Natasha.

To top things off, another student couple who had a baby during this time named their baby girl Rosemary after the other short-term missionary who served alongside me. In Sukuma culture, babies are often named after their grandparents, so after baby Natasha was born, people began to call me *Bibi* (which means grandmother in Swahili).

To celebrate the birth of new babies, the mamas come together to give the babies and their parents a blessing ceremony. I will never forget Natasha's baby blessing. It was a hot Saturday in February and Mama Nangale and I walked twenty minutes from our homes, toward the water, with me taking video of baby goats (kids), cows, and sheep that were walking through the village. Timothy and his wife lived near the lake, and when we arrived there was a table, several rows of wooden church pews, and a blue tarp on the grass outside of their small brick house. I headed over to the tarp to play with two little girls, Precious and Praise, the daughters of one of my first-year diploma students.

Soon, the ladies began filling the empty seats, and the program's officiants took their places in the front of the yard at the table where a small Bible and a red Swahili hymn book were resting. I absolutely loved attending events with the mamas, who were mostly students in the Swahili-speaking Christian Ministry women's program at the Bible college. They could barely understand me and me them, but we bonded and I genuinely loved these African queens. They were the sweetest ladies, who cooked delicious food, prayed and sang beautifully, and always attempted to hold conversations with me as they displayed great patience without getting frustrated with our language barriers. After chatting and greeting one another for several minutes, their husbands, who were mostly theology students and ministers, arrived and sat on logs on the grass behind the mamas. A few ladies stayed behind in a nearby home preparing lunch and making tea.

There was lots of singing, dancing, laughing, and drinking chai-chai. My favorite part of this event was participating in the Sukuma traditional blessings. After praying over baby Natasha, one mama shouted a chorus and everyone else joined in with singing, dancing, and clapping. The baby was then passed around to each person as we sang over her, prayed over her, and danced around the yard. It was beautiful, and it symbolized the community's blessing for this new baby.

I can still remember the joy that overcame me and everyone there as we held the baby that day blessing the life that God had prepared for her. I had never witnessed such a communal display of love for a new baby. In America, we traditionally host baby showers for expectant parents prior to babies being born, but once the newborn arrives, for Christians, baby dedications (or blessings) often consist of the babies being taken before the church, and the family receiving prayer. Babies may be sprinkled with water as a symbolism of their dedication to Christ, however, nothing so communal and close-knit as in Africa. In America, I have never seen a mother willingly allow several people to hold, dance, and sing over her new baby.

Baby Natasha was close to two months old by the time her baby blessing took place, but she was still quite small. Even when she was first born, the community of mamas gathered around the family to help them with their new bundle of joy. Everyone held her, sang, and prayed over her. Natasha's mama would bring her to our class and to chapel. Natasha was so mild-mannered and calm, and I never saw her shed a tear. Most new moms I know from home will not allow people, outside of immediate family, to hold and touch babies and are often very apprehensive about taking children out when they are newborns.

While I was in Tanzania, Felicia, one of my best friends for over two decades, gave birth to her first son. While I could not see baby Caleb in person even when I came home, due to the COVID-19 pandemic, Felicia has always been one to keep everyone in her village in the loop about the latest happenings in her life. Each month, she would send a recap video of Caleb's growth with pictures and special moments. It has been beautiful to see him grow and the joy he is bringing to his family. Around the time when Caleb was born, Felicia's husband's sister passed away. Caleb's grandparents lost one of their children. The pictures Felicia and her husband would send Caleb's grandparents were the light they needed in a dark tunnel after losing a child amidst a pandemic. Felicia mentioned that she regularly received messages from her family about how Caleb was the one bright spot during this time.

As I reflected on the baby blessings ceremonies, the joy we experienced in the village with the birth of the new babies, and the excitement of watching baby Caleb grow, I was reminded of what the Word of God tells us about babies. They are gifts from the Lord, an inheritance to families, and blessing to the villages to which they belong.

> **"Behold, children are a heritage from the Lord, the fruit of the womb a reward."**
>
> Psalm 127:3

> **"When a woman is giving birth, she has sorrow because her hour has come, but when she has delivered the baby, she no longer remembers the anguish, for joy that a human being has been born into the world."**
>
> John 16:21

> **"See that you do not despise one of these little ones. For I tell you that in heaven their angels always see the face of my Father who is in heaven."**
>
> Matthew 18:10

> **"But when Jesus saw it, he was indignant and said to them, 'Let the children come to me; do not hinder them, for to such belongs the kingdom of God.'"**
>
> Mark 10:14

Baby Blessings Journal Reflection:

From this chapter and the scriptures above we see that children are not only a blessing to parents and families, but to their entire communities. Do you view the children who you have birthed or who are in your life as a blessing to those who come in contact with them? In what ways can you instill this same attitude in others around you? How do you teach the children in your life their self-worth and value at a young age?

CHAPTER 16

they shall be comforted

"Bear one another's burdens, and thereby fulfill the law of Christ."

Galatians 6:2

I was in my classroom later than usual, around 3 p.m. on one of my first afternoons on the campus. Several students came in my room and mentioned that it was time for them to go to "comfort" another student. I didn't know what they meant by comforting him, and I assumed these were his friends and were going to pay him a visit, be kind, and offer encouraging words. It wasn't until about twenty minutes later when I was on my way home and saw two staff members on the dirt road to my house. They said, "We're going to comfort Kahensa."

"What is going on there? I heard some people were going to comfort him. Am I supposed to be going," I asked.

Musa, another teacher said, "Yes, you should really be there, but since you're new it's probably okay that you do not attend." By now, I was curious. Although I still had no idea what comforting would entail, I decided to go. I tightened my heavy book bag on my back, and I along with the other two teachers walked down the dirt road to the student housing area where a large crowd was already gathered around sitting on lawn chairs. On the way to the comfort service, I learned that Kahensa's mom had passed away during the summer.

I quickly realized this comfort service was a cross between the American version of funerals and repasts that take place after funeral services. Only, comfort services do not occur the same day. The family, which included my student, his wife, and their four children, sat in the front of the crowd. There was a small table and a basket to collect monetary contributions there. The school's principal was sitting in the front row with a Swahili Bible in hand. The evangelistic singers stood up after a while and began to sing. Unlike the normal smiles, exuberant dances, and coordinated dresses and shirts the singers often wore when they performed, their garments and body expressions told a story of sorrow this time. The women were dressed in casual t-shirts and wore kitenge around their waists. Their movements were stiff and their faces were straight. Their body expressions mimicked the sad nature of the occasion. After they sang a few songs, the preacher for the event, a fourth year student, began to share a message, similar to a eulogy. Musa, who was sitting beside me took this opportunity to translate for me while also telling me what was happening. After the message was delivered, the family stood up and Kahensa began to share his mother's "obituary" in Swahili, only there were no printed programs or bios to read from. He spoke from his heart about his mom. Afterwards, the family thanked everyone. Then, the singers began to perform another song while everyone, who was able, went to the front where the collection basket was held and put in money for the family. Afterwards, some of the student-organizers passed out fresh, hot peanuts and steaming hot lemongrass tea with leaves picked from Abram and Ashby's yard. It was still September and very dry and hot outside, probably close to ninety-five degrees. As I mentioned, I was still new to the country and not used to the customs. I just couldn't understand why we were drinking steaming hot tea in what felt like one thousand degree weather. Although it was delicious, I began to sweat even more. Later, I realized that it is custom to drink *chai chai* (lemongrass tea) at gatherings. After we were done eating and drinking, the comfort service was over, and many of the students in attendance began to stack the chairs, collect the plastic tea cups and small pieces of plastic where the peanuts had been wrapped.

During my time in Tanzania, many people transitioned. During my first experience with the comfort service, it was quite unique and even bitter sweet. Kahensa grew up in a Muslim family, and after he received the Lord, Kahensa was given a choice to either choose Christ or leave his family and live as an exile away from home. A young Kahensa, brave yet filled with trepidation, chose Christ. He left his home on foot and lived alone during what he referred to as a wilderness season, until finally meeting another Christian who directed him to a village where he would be accepted and helped by other believers. After a few years, his dad sent someone to find him and asked him to return home. Long story short, Kahensa has made it his life's mission to lead his clan to Christ. Several of his siblings have converted and even his mom received the Lord prior to her death. Although sad to lose his mother, my student found great peace with his mom's death because she had received Jesus not long before she died.

After celebrating the life of Kahensa's mom and comforting the mourning family, it wasn't long before the father-in-law of another student passed. Then, the next death came as a sudden tragedy to a close neighbor who received a call around 6 a.m. one morning that her father had suddenly died. She was not expecting this and had to quickly gather the funds to travel by bus to her home village. The funeral was planned for the day after his death. This young mother and student in our school's women's program was visibly broken by this news and probably even more stressed to know her husband would need to take care of their five children alone while she was away from Bulima burying her father. She returned to campus after a couple of weeks, and we held a comfort service for her.

~

To me, death seemed to hit this village more frequently than I was used to in my home country, especially for us to be living in such a small community. The life expectancy in Tanzania is between sixty-six and sixty-eight years old, compared to about seventy-nine in America, eighty-one in the UK, and eighty-two in Canada. I believe this younger life expectancy is partly due to the lack of access to good healthcare and adequate medical treatment. Economic disparities in developing nations affect every part of life in these countries, even death. I've heard stories of how Tanzanians often do not go to the hospital at the onset of illness, often because of finances, and by the time many people seek medical treatment it is already too late.

As time went on, people continued to transition. The college's chaplain lost her father and the father-in-law of Peter, a student in Inductive Bible Study, also transitioned. Many others died in the village also. Some nights, the town crier (as I referred to him) would interrupt the nightly solace with his megaphone to share the details of yet another death in the village and an accompanying funeral service to memorialize the person. These announcements were in Swahili, of course, so I usually had to get an update the next day from one of my teacher colleagues. On the ride into the city one Friday, I remember seeing a crowd of at least two hundred people sitting outside and gathering into a church. The crowd spilled over into the nearby road. They were there for a funeral.

Funeral scenes and preparation, comfort services, and prayers for the sick were a regular part of life. I grew very close to many of my students and would pray with them for their relatives quite often. They would often visit my home, talk to me about their plans, and share details about their families. I'd visit their homes and share a delicious meal with their families, talk, laugh, and dance with babies and children. On Sundays, they all had ministry assignments, and I'd stop in to visit some of them as they ministered as well. I spent a lot of time with the diploma class because I taught them more than any other group. One day, during the all-school chapel service, a young man from that class, Yohana, asked everyone to pray that his mother would be healed. She was gravely ill in the hospital with little sign of hope. During the course of that week, he and his best friend, Peter, (who was in the same class) started to text me asking for me to pray specifically and fervently for his mom because her condition worsened by the day. More chapel announcements were shared about her dire condition and we prayed more. The diploma class even interceded during class, and one night I sent the best friends healing scriptures to speak over his mom. After encouraging the two young men to remain in faith, I was devastated to awake the following morning to find text messages from them both. Yohana's mother had transitioned in the wee hours of the night/early morning. This news was devastating because I know he wasn't ready or prepared to lose his mom. Who is ever prepared for the death of a parent? My heart shattered, and I had a tough time teaching that day.

That same morning, I taught this group for our Personal Spiritual Development class. To my surprise Yohana came to class, and several of us fought back tears as we prayed for him as he prepared to leave the class when his piki arrived to take him to the bus stop. This hurt especially because his mom was a pastor's wife who had just given birth to a baby less than a year before. Over the next few hours and days, I personally witnessed how his nine classmates pulled together to comfort him. This was one of the sincerest demonstrations of love that I witnessed. Although he had already left Bulima for Mwanza, his friends and classmates, brothers and sisters in Christ, put their money together and sought support from teachers for bus fare to the funeral service and a monetary contribution for the family. I could see the love of Christ in each of them as they shared in the pain and heartbreak of their friend and brother.

This experience caused me to reflect on a passage from Romans chapter 12 when the Apostle Paul teaches the church how to demonstrate their love. He exhorts believers to have sincere love, hate what is evil, cling to what is good, be devoted to each other in love, and honor others above oneself. Then he directs his readers to rejoice with those who rejoice and mourn with those who mourn (verse 15). I witnessed the students mourn with their classmate with sincerity. During the weeks after this young mama's passing, I could see this class grow closer and a few of the friends who were particularly close were hardly ever seen apart.

Simplicity in Saying Goodbye

One major difference in the processes of memorializing the deceased and comforting mourning families in Tanzania and America is that for the former, the dead are laid to rest really quickly. The process seems very simple. The wooden caskets are purchased ready to use with a cross or some other Christian figure carved on the top. While riding down the two-hour stretch of road to Mwanza through many of the villages on the way, you are bound to see several caskets for sale by local entrepreneurs.

The funeral processes that I've seen and have been involved in at home are more intricate than the simple gatherings with food, music, singing, and preaching in the village. In America, families can spend days selecting the best casket, putting together a typed obituary, figuring out the arrangements for the body such as burial or cremation, funeral homes and cemeteries, who will deliver the eulogy, keep the ashes, floral arrangements, and whose insurance company will pay for it all. Funerals can cost close to fifteen thousand dollars or more. In Tanzania, I saw families and friends gather, memorialize their loved ones, praise God, eat, and receive support from their communities. Love to the mourning family and respect for the deceased happens within a much simpler, less-expensive process in Tanzania.

The Bible college where I serve has a procedure to host comfort services for those who mourn. Most of the comfort services are held in the school's chapel, especially when the mourning student or faculty member lives in the dorm instead of a house. When the grieving individual lives in a house in the village, the comfort service is often held outside of that home as was the case for Kahensa. I've mentioned this before, but although life in this village is simple, there is a sweetness about it that I have not seen anywhere else. Many of the customs and traditions practiced here are so very Biblical and have made me also evaluate the prevalence of Biblical values in my own culture.

Think back for a moment about the story of Jesus' friend Lazarus' death in the New Testament book of John chapter eleven. When Jesus arrived to Bethany after Lazarus had been in the tomb for four days, the Bible tells us in John 11:19, " . . .many Jews had come to Martha and Mary to comfort them in the loss of their brother." The Bible documents a first-century comfort service in the village of Bethany, a service that Jesus did not fully make it to before the sisters met him en route (vs. 30). What is very clear about this passage was that the people in attendance were very focused and committed to comforting the sisters. Verse 31 says, "When the Jews who had been with Mary in the house, comforting her (some versions say consoling), noticed how quickly she got up and went out, they followed her, supposing she was going to the tomb to mourn there."

As I explored this concept of comforting a bit more, I realized that the comfort services in the village are the literal manifestation of what was demonstrated in this passage and what Jesus taught in Matthew chapter five in the sermon on the mount:

Now when Jesus saw the crowds, he went up on a mountainside and sat down. His disciples came to him, and he began to teach them. He said "Blessed are the poor in spirit, for theirs is the kingdom of heaven. Blessed are those who mourn, for they will be comforted."

Matthew 5:1-4

In the Sermon on the Mount, Jesus taught his hearers how to behave as kingdom citizens. This sermon included the blessings for disciples who are afflicted and humble: those poor in spirit, those who mourn, those who hunger and thirst for righteousness, the meek, the merciful, the pure in heart, the peacemakers, those who are persecuted for righteousness, the insulted, and the wrongfully accused. Each group suffers and receives a heavenly reward. Comfort is the heavenly reward for those who mourn. In fact, the Holy Spirit, who is the gift from God to believers everywhere is referred to as The Comforter. In John 14:26, Jesus reassured his disciples of this gift of comfort by saying:

> **But the Helper (Comforter, Advocate, Intercessor—Counselor, Strengthener, Standby), the Holy Spirit, whom the Father will send in My name [in My place, to represent Me and act on My behalf], He will teach you all things. And He will help you remember everything that I have told you.**
>
> John 14:26 (Amplified Bible)

Today in Bulima and in villages, cities, and towns everywhere, the Holy Spirit's indwelling in believers acts as a comforter to people who mourn. While the comfort services in Tanzania made me think deeper about the idea of comfort and what it means, Western cultures are not without their own traditions. For instance, when my maternal grandmother transitioned in January of 2018, many family members from across the country flew into Kansas all within a few days of the sad news to comfort one another, plan, and attend her funeral. The church in Junction City, Kansas where my grandmother had served most of her life offered us their church for the wake and many of the church mothers prepared food that was already out when we arrived at the church for the repast. Often, death brings people together in a way that life could not. Although different in style and execution, the American traditions of funerals and repasts are important events in the cycle of life that we should treat with holy sensitivity. I believe there is also an opportunity for us to glean from the African tradition of supporting mourning families, by embedding comfort services into major institutions that serve as home for its members during significant parts of their lives, including boarding schools, colleges, and universities. In Bulima, there's a spirit of community embedded within the culture, a sense of relationships and every day, intentional efforts to help meet the needs of fellow believers.

Be it through comfort services or monetary contributions, it all boils down to their intentional desire to walk in the Word, follow the example of Christ Jesus, and do as he commanded, which in this case is to comfort those who mourn.

Comfort Action and Journal:

Due to the fast pace of Western society, social media, social distancing (new reality as of 2020), and hardness of our cultures which often turns into hardness of heart, we can easily overlook or become immune to the pain that others may be feeling. This week, be intentional about comforting others and showing compassion to those who are hurting. Document these encounters in your journal. How do people respond to your intentional efforts to comfort them?

PART 4

cultural
spiritual
transformation

CHAPTER 17

the west DOES NOT save the rest

"For if the willingness is there, the gift is acceptable according to what one has, not according to what one does not have."

2 Corinthians 8:12

Mama Nangale started out as my Swahili instructor in September of 2019. We met for lessons at my dining room table three days a week. We instantly connected and she became like a mother figure to me; she helped me navigate through village life, communicate with neighbors in Swahili because that is the primary language of those who live in Bulima, and make friends. She accompanied me on some of my ministry engagements and taught me how to cook like Tanzanians.

On my second mission trip, my budget was extremely limited. The mission was not funded at even thirty percent so the entire trip was a faith move. I knew God had called me to return because my heart was there, and I knew that's where I belonged in that season of my life. During my second term, because of the limited budget, I had to cut back on my Swahili lessons and many other expenses.

One afternoon as Mama Nangale and I cleaned beans in her backyard, I expressed the deep sadness that I felt with not being able to help the many students who needed school fees or even the sick children and students who contracted malaria or other illnesses on a weekly basis and who needed medicine from the dispensary.

In the moment when I felt my lowest, Mama Nangale looked at me firmly and said, "Maybe it's your time to receive." A sudden peace overtook me and I knew the Holy Spirit was speaking through her. It was a revelation that challenged my ideas of what God wanted to accomplish through me during the mission trip. As a missionary from the West, I left home for a cross-culture experience with a mindset of helping, serving, and giving. Upon arriving, I realized I could never address every need. I also realized there was a two-way work of the Holy Spirit happening where me, the missionary, was being transformed just as much as those I was serving.

During this season, I experienced an awakening in part because the people I was there to help ended up giving me their lives and teaching me more than I could have ever imagined. I know I am not the only person who has experienced this. Mama Nangale was right. It was my time to receive, but not in a material sense. It was my time to receive God's peace and love through his beautiful people. It was my time to receive a new perspective and depart from the mentality that I always had to be the problem solver and solution finder. Those former ways of thinking had to go, and instead I was being called to experience joy in the sweet friendships and opportunities to connect with people on a deeper level. It was my time to receive a new revelation of giving that equated to giving one's life. It was also my time to receive new relationships that were not centered on what I could offer, but instead, what we could offer one another which was God's love. Would my neighbors receive me and I them if I had nothing to give except myself? Could we become real friends without the possibility of financial exchanges? Could we enjoy true fellowship once my neighbors learned that I would not be able to meet as many of their physical needs as they had hoped? When they heard, "I'm sorry, I can't . . ." or "I don't have the budget for that . . ." would they still come to visit and sit with me? "Are the people of Bulima just as loving to missionaries when missionaries cannot give financially?" These were some of the tough questions that I pondered and to which I would receive my answer.

In addition to all of these questions and revelations, in hindsight, I've been able to recognize more of what God was doing strategically in that season. For years, I had struggled with people pleasing and remnants of the spirit of rejection. I didn't realize how deep the people pleasing ran until I got to the mission field and found myself doing things or giving money without inquiring of the Lord because others asked me for it and I didn't want them to think I was selfish. I found myself giving pretty much all of my money away for the week until I realized, "Oh, I need to stop. I may need this last 10,000 shillings (approximately seven American dollars)." No one knew, but even after I knew I did not have an excess to give, I still did, and I would leave myself with 10,000 shillings or less until the next Friday when I could get funds from the ATM in Mwanza.

In the absence of an excess of funds during my second missionary journey to Tanzania, I had to trust God to multiply the little that I had. And he did, with great measure. In addition to this, God was giving me a perspective of what it was like to live and be like the people who I served amongst. Many people who will read this book will never experience poverty or the lack of financial abundance. Many will never live in a surrendered place of fully trusting God to provide without having the security of a job, residual income, a savings account, or relatives who can help make ends meet. When you do not have these securities to depend on, the luxuries that you do have become so important and valuable. That, for me, was my relationship with God and his people.

That day in Mama Nangale's backyard, she suggested that I remain honest with people about my support and finances and they would understand, but what I remember most is the way she looked at me and explained that it was okay for me to receive. In the end, God provided more than I bargained for. I think he wanted me to reach a place where I trusted him completely. I never lacked. I was able to help people, support students, and give to sick children, although my giving looked much different during the second term. Thanks to supporters who desired to invest in Tanzanians, we were able to help student pastors, widows, and orphans as well.

Despite what the Lord gave these neighbors, as he funneled resources through me, I received much more than the physical help that came from my hands. My neighbors gave me themselves in many ways. God used them to meet every need that I had and many that I didn't know existed. That's the thing about life. Often we don't realize what is missing until we receive it and can't imagine living without it. For me, that missing piece was another layer of God's love.

The West Saves the Rest

For years in the missionary culture, there was this attitude and belief system that "the West saves the rest." This is because for five centuries, the West was the primary sender of missionaries. This attitude perpetuated the idea that beyond spiritual salvation, Western missionaries went to other nations to save them both spiritually and financially. Because this notion has been embedded in the fabric of many societies and publicized widely through media and other means, many people in developing nations think of those from the west as endless wells of financial resources. Spiritually speaking, this epithet is no longer true. The West is also a missions field. In 2019, a Gallup poll reported that the number of people who attend church regularly was down to half, which was a twenty percent decrease since 1999.

> U.S. church membership was seventy percent or higher from 1937 through 1976, falling modestly to an average of sixty-eight percent in the 1970s through the 1990s. The past twenty years have seen an acceleration in the drop-off, with a twenty-percentage-point decline since 1999 and more than half of that change occurring since the start of the current decade . . . The decline in church membership mostly reflects

the fact that fewer Americans than in the past now have any religious affiliation. However, even those who do identify with a particular religion are less likely to belong to a church or other place of worship than in the past.[26]

Today, missionaries actually come to America from other countries. Our backyards are missions fields as New Age beliefs and other religions are on the rise, there are more opportunities to share the gospel. As one of my good friends from seminary, who is a young man in his twenties and recently appointed chaplain at a federal prison put it, "Many young people and black men want to be anything but Christian." He noted the rise in the Black Hebrew Israelite movement within Federal prisons.

The primary reason I wanted to write this chapter is because I believe those of us who live missional can help change "the west saves the rest" narrative. Through this work, I want to demonstrate that the spirituality that we are so accustomed to in the West could use a bit of resuscitation that can be found in cultures like my beloved village in Tanzania. When we stop looking at and behaving like our missions fields both home and abroad are charity cases, and instead get into a posture of being willing to receive and listen, we can see that in fact we need each other. I cannot explain to you how many times God uses people who need the love of Jesus to meet a need that I have. Where our excessive and overly booked schedules, smart phones, and crime rates have created hard shells around our hearts, the humanity of villages or even poverty-stricken cities can allow our faith to be re-grounded in what really matters, and that is the mission of God. God so loved the world that he sent his Son to save us all. Jesus himself declared that he came for those on the margins of society. The margins exist everywhere. We are all subject to the margins, and therefore, we can never allow a savior complex to take root within us as we serve Christ. We are not the Savior, we serve the Savior.

---

26. Jeffrey M. Jones, "U.S. Church Membership Down Sharply in Past Two Decades," Gallop, April 18, 2019, https://news.gallup.com/poll/248837/church-membership-down-sharply-past-two-decades.aspx.

We must fight against the pride and arrogance that permeates our Christian cultures, and instead see ourselves and each other from the eyes of God.

The West Does Not Save the Rest Prayer:

Dear Heavenly Father, I pray that the reader of this book would humbly receive from you, however that may come. I pray, Lord, that you break down the walls in his or her heart; remove the arrogance and pride; eliminate the need to perform, to always be the one who provides solutions, so that he or she can also receive from those who seemingly have less. Lord lift every burden placed on him or her that is not from you because your burden is light. Lord, allow this person to become a contagious Christian who multiplies the body of Christ and makes disciples that behave and love like Jesus. In the name of Jesus we thank you and pray, amen.

CHAPTER 18

life givers (prayer, knowledge, burdens, feasts, and friends)

**"Greater love has no one than this, that someone lay down his
life for his friends."**

John 15:13 ESV

I n more ways than one, living in Bulima expanded my thoughts
about giving and gave me a new understanding of what the
Bible teaches. Too often, when we hear messages about giving
from the pulpit, they are focused on financial gifts. However,
this is not the full revelation, or even the main revelation, of giving in the Bible. We are instructed, instead, to lay down (give)
our lives for our friends (John 15:13). In fact, life giving is the
example that God set forth for us from the very beginning. We
see this play out starting with creation, in the Garden of Eden,
through the Old Testament with God's unending mercy for the
disobedient and rebellious Israelites, and throughout the New
Testament and beyond with the incarnation, crucifixion, and
resurrection of Jesus to provide eternal life to believers. We also
see sacrificial living and the giving of life as we read through the
gospels, Acts, and the epistles and see examples of disciples and
apostles leaving all to boldly follow and serve Jesus. It is very
clear that as children made in his image (Gen. 1:26), God desires
our lives.

As a good Father, God does not require from us what he does not first demonstrate. God so loved the world that he *gave* his only begotten Son (John 3:16). Jesus came to give us an abundant life (John 10:10). During his earthly ministry, Jesus restored life to those who were sick, demon possessed, lame, and in sin. He did this by offering his gifts of healing, wisdom, fellowship, and hope to ensure his followers lived in complete freedom, despite the world's evils. Christ went to the cross and suffered crucifixion, giving his life for our pain, suffering, transgressions, iniquities, punishment, healing, and salvation (Isaiah 53). When Christ resurrected from the grave, he continued to give us life—this time he arose with all power and authority over the devil and provided us this same victory (Col. 2:15, 1 Cor. 15:57). But not only that, Christ gave us life in the Spirit, which empowers us to live the life he died on the cross to give us. The Bible tells us that as Christ was, so are we in this world, (1 John 4:17), therefore, it is very clear that God desires our complete surrender and availability to lay down our lives for others as he has for us.

During my second term, I taught a class on the book of 1 John to third-year students. In this course, we talked extensively about the biblical definition of love. The Apostle John is known as the "Apostle of Love," and he echoed his sentiments from the gospels in 1 John 3:16 when he wrote, "By this we know love, because He laid down His life for us. And we also ought to lay down *our* lives for the brethren" (NKJV). According to the Apostle John, the proof of God's love for us is that he *gave* his Son to be the propitiation for our sins (1 John 4:10). So you see, giving our lives for others is the expectation and standard for believers of Christ.

While in the village, I learned so much from my neighbors about this concept. Giving took on a new meaning. It was not only about monetary factors, resources, or time; but how all of those gifts play a bigger role in the act of giving one's life. I came to understand giving in terms of the act of giving life, aside from money, things, and material possessions. Regardless of what they do or do not have, my neighbors in the village give what is invaluable and impossible to measure in quantifiable terms. The longer I spent in the village, the more I was able to witness God's biblical standard of living and giving in action in many important areas. I believe that as we review the examples of life-giving from the people of Bulima and the Bible college community, the Holy Spirit will speak to our hearts about our own giving and if there is room for us to become more like Christ.

#1: Life-giving Prayer

"Pray without Ceasing."

1 Thessalonians 5:16

"Praying at all times in the Spirit, with all prayer and supplication. To that end keep alert with all perseverance, making supplication for all the saints . . ."

Ephesians 6:18

Upon returning home, my good friend Lyndon helped me to put words around the prayer lives of the neighbors in the village. When Christians in Bulima and many communities outside of the Western hemisphere pray, they are often praying for needs that can be met by no one other than God. Prayers often center around sufficient rain to provide nourishment for crops so that there is enough food for families, or that locusts would not consume all of their harvest. They pray for the financial provision to rebuild a roof on a house that blew off when the latest storm ravaged through the village, and for sick children to get well despite not having the proper medication or medical access. Another common prayer is for basic needs of financially strapped families and students. My friend Lyndon explained these needs require God's intervention, whereas, often in Western cultures we pray for enough money to add luxuries to our lives like new and upgraded homes and cars, higher-paying jobs, the ability to pamper ourselves, or scrape up the funds we need to join our friends on vacation. These are non-essential prayer needs, which means that when they are not answered, there is no substantial effect. For most people, basic needs are taken care of, which is not the case in many countries like Tanzania. I am not discounting the real needs within the entire Western world, because homelessness, poverty, and economic disparities exist here in abundance as well. I am speaking of the desperation in prayer that believers in Tanzania demonstrate. Furthermore, because they don't typically follow Christ or serve in the church for monetary gain, popularity, or social notoriety which is common in the West, there is a level of purity that we find in their prayer lives. For our neighbors in Bulima, prayer is not something to be taken lightly or prioritized behind anything else.

One day as I was writing this book while still in the village, I heard a faint, "Hodi," at the door. The pastor's wife and two of their sons were standing on the porch. The three came in, and Mama barely spoke English so the older son, Nelia, translated as per his usual routine. He said, "Madam we've come to pray with you before we go home." It was pretty much dark outside. They didn't ask if they could pray for me or if I had prayer needs, they simply told me why they were there because of course I had prayer needs. *Everyone always has prayer needs.* After our sweet time together, my heart warmed and I was comforted by the fact that they took the time to come and pray with me. One of the best parts of living in the village was that I knew that I was not forgotten by my neighbors. They were always praying for me and all the saints.

I grew accustomed to unexpected visitors at any time of the day: village girls selling produce, a church member fundraising for a building project, or one of my students asking me to explain an assignment. However, the same was true for visitors who simply wanted to pray with me. This was not abnormal. If me or my neighboring missionary were sick and students learned of this, they would come to our home, insist on praying and reading the scriptures. On this particular evening, the pastor's family came to pray, not because I had any specific needs nor had I requested prayer. Perhaps Mama was familiar with Ephesians 6:18 or 1 Thessalonians 5:16. Prayer became the most essential part of my mission. Oswald Chambers said, "Prayer does not fit us for the greater work; prayer is the greater work." This is definitely true for missionaries. As I've reread my journals from my time in Bulima, most of what I wrote was prayer related: prayer needs in the village and school, prayer needs for loved ones back home, prayer items that came up as a result of reading Scripture or talking with neighbors, and direct prayers to God that I wanted to repeatedly pray. I knew that God had called me to the ministry of prayer, but in Bulima, surrounded by prayer warriors, I believe God birthed an intercessor in me.

There is no way that a missionary can be fruitful (and healthy) without a prayer life and without others committed to interceding for him or her in prayer as well. I recently read a book by David Early called *Prayer: The Timeless Secret of High-Impact Leaders,* and he has an entire chapter on soliciting the prayers of others. It's actually called "Train Others to Pray for You." He tells the story of how early in his ministry he overlooked the importance of soliciting prayers from his community. Then one day, he woke up with sharp pains, welts, and twenty-two boils all over his arms and legs. He went to the doctor, who could not pinpoint what could be wrong with Early. The doctor, who was a believer, told him he had never seen anything like it except in the book of Job. Immediately, a lightbulb went off in the doctor's head and he asked Early, "What are you preaching about on Sunday?" Early was preaching a sermon on spiritual warfare. He went home. His wife called prayer warriors and solicited their prayers, and in a few days the boils were completely gone. The prayers of the righteous are powerful and effective, and we need others to pray for us, especially when we are in ministry!

In Bulima, the directive to "pray without ceasing," took on a new meaning. I prayed more with others than I ever had in my life. I witnessed prayer as a vital part of the public life here, which is quite different from what I had experienced before this. In America, many believers talk about their prayer lives, but aside from social media and corporate church gatherings many communities lack public, spontaneous prayer. I have never experienced a neighbor coming to my house and telling me that they wanted to pray for me. We aren't as friendly or relational, so it's not normal for someone to randomly walk up to your door to simply tell you they want to pray (except for maybe Jehovah's Witnesses). Perhaps this is something that we should get back to.

One day, after one of my classes where I ministered on the supernatural power of God to heal and provide miracles, a student named Daniel, asked if we could all pray together. Another classmate mentioned that his sister was set to get heart surgery in a couple days. We prayed fervently for the sister and later learned that while we were praying, she felt heat in her chest. A few days later, she returned to get x-rays prior to having surgery, and the doctors could no longer find any issues that would indicate a need for heart surgery. We knew that God had provided a miracle. Throughout Scripture we see that God has already done everything for us that He will ever do. Jesus' finished work on the cross contains the promises for all that we need. Ephesians 1:3 tells us that God has already released everything we need. With this in mind, I saw how prayer and faith put us in the position to receive everything God has provided including healing of the heart of my student's sister. There is no way to access the promises of God without prayer.

One day Mwalimu Nangale engaged me in a conversation at the school library, and he told me that he knew I was a prayer warrior, and he wanted us to have a prayer meeting at his house. A few days later, he, Mama Nangale and I spent a couple of hours interceding for the nations, our respective countries, families, and the school. Mwalimu had a prayer agenda and we followed his lead. I knew that someone in Tanzania was always praying for me while I was there, and even after I left, I knew that there were people praying for me seven thousand miles away. It rubbed off on me. When I came home, I became more fervent in my prayer and fasting life and also resumed a prayer meeting and podcast that I had started, the Victory Prayer Circle, which has a group of intercessors that had remained active while I was in Tanzania. As you may recall, at one point, I felt like nobody was praying for me. That was in November during my first missionary journey. When I returned to Tanzania, God made sure that I knew people were praying for me, but he also allowed them to become a great influence on my life as an intercessor! Today, I continue to pray for my friends in the village and the believers in Tanzania and I believe that they continue to pray for me. I was thankful to get connected to a group of Tanzanians in America to continue interceding for my neighbors in the village, and share my life with them through prayer. Intercession is one way we can give our lives for others.

#2: Knowledge and Wisdom

"A generous person will prosper; whoever refreshes others will be refreshed."

Proverbs 11:25

The word for *refreshes* means water in the Hebrew, which is defined as to saturate, fill, satiate, and satisfy. At a theological college, one of the top ways to satiate or satisfy someone, besides the presence of God, is to provide tools and resources to help one learn and grow closer to God and life purpose.

Mwalimu Nangale and I share a love for books and teaching. He began stopping me on the road or meeting me at school with books or questions about books that I've read. One day, he gave me a little black book with a torn brown book cover. Its contents? *David Brainerd, Man of Prayer* by Oswald J. Smith. I assumed Mwalimu gave me the book assuming it could help me as I had mentioned to him that I was in the middle of a twenty-one day fast. Brainerd was a missionary to India who devoted his life to fasting and prayer. This book was such an on-time read for me, and I was grateful for Mwalimu. I read most of it in just one night and became so inspired to even write this book again and set goals for finishing it. The next week, Mwalimu Nangale brought me *Spiritual Leadership* by Henry and Richard Blackaby, which I had started reading before the holiday; four leadership books by John Maxwell, including Maxwell's *The 21 Irrefutable Laws of Leadership*. My only disappointment was that my teaching schedule didn't allow me the time to complete all of the books he would share with me on a weekly basis.

Mwalimu wasn't the only person to share his wisdom. His son, Musa, is a tech specialist who also enjoys reading. He and I exchanged books, computer knowledge, and he helped get me acclimated to life in the village (as did all of my neighbors) by sharing many of the customs and even the language with me. Mama Nangale, with the help of Musa, was my Swahili teacher, and she also taught me about cultivating food. The Kidds, full-term missionaries, also helped me understand and communicate with others and taught me about the "big city" Mwanza, and the ins and outs of shopping in the city. I learned a great deal about missionary culture from them and my neighboring missionary, Rosemary, who has served as a missionary for over forty years. My neighbor, Enoch, has become a great friend. He's a graphic designer who helps me with my business and even designed this book cover. My students Daniel, Lucas, Simon, Peter, Rioba, Isack, Mariam, Yohana, John, Naomi, Aneth, Sarah, and many others visited me regularly to give me their insights and revelation from the Bible, their classes, lives, businesses, and dreams. I learned so much from everyone there, and their willingness to share their wisdom reflected the heart of God.

As they all shared their wisdom with me, I also shared some of my own customs and traditions with them. I shared books, authors, and revelations that I'd receive. My students were the primary recipients of course, but both in and outside of the classroom, I saw how the mutual love and giving mentality advanced our collective work. This may not seem like a big deal or a point worth mentioning, but the Bible tells us that people perish for a lack of knowledge (or revelation). Sometimes, in America at least, people can claim to be a friend or someone with our best interests at heart, yet they will withhold information that can better us. I've grown to really value the opportunity to both share and receive knowledge with others. We should all aim to shorten the learning curve for someone else. I sometimes wonder what my life as a first-time missionary would have been like had I not been placed in Bulima with people who willingly strived to shorten my learning curve.

I know that God is strategic and the moments of fellowship through sharing knowledge was intentionally designed by him.

#3 Burdens

"Bear one another's burdens, and so fulfill the law of Christ."

Galatians 6:2

In the New Testament, the Greek word used for *burdens* means heaviness, weight (load), or trouble, according to Strong's Bible Dictionary. True friends, brothers and sisters in the Spirit share in each other's burdens (Galatians 6:2-3). This simple command can be downplayed as simply "Christianese," but we can and should live this out with intentionality. We fulfill this command by walking in love, listening during hardships, and helping others fulfill the responsibilities that they have.

In her book, *The Courage to Identify Who You Are,* my friend and author Sharon Angel describes a time when she was in so much emotional anguish that she needed a friend in that moment. When her friend arrived at her home, Sharon was laying on the floor in tears. Her friend crawled down on the floor right beside her, comforted her, and shared in that moment of anguish. Whenever I hear Sharon talk about this moment, I can picture it and can visibly see the love and life of that moment. This can give us a visual of what it looks like to share others' burdens.

Merriam-Webster dictionary defines *burden* as a load, duty, or responsibility, something oppressive or worrisome, or the bearing of a load. In Bulima, when students cross paths with teachers, they take their teachers' bags or books for as long as they walk together. Mamas would come over to help me cook or clean or fix something that was broken. I remember one day, our power was out and I had a Swahili lesson with Mama Nangale. She came over and asked if I had water stored up because the power had been out in our village for several hours and no one knew when it would return. Mama Nangale told me about the times when there was no power for days and the water supply shut off. She explained that we quickly needed to store water for me in the house before it ran out. For the next hour, we proceeded to fill up several buckets, basins, and water bottles with faucet water. She even took me to her house and showed me how much water she had stored and gave me an extra bucket to use. She could have kept quiet and let me continue to have my few measly water bottles and that's it. Instead, she cared enough to show me the correct way to prepare. The two times my kitchen sink broke, Buto, the brilliant village handyman and engineer was at my house within minutes to gladly fix it, (even on a Sunday). Neighbors in Bulima shared burdens and responsibilities, helped to bear the loads of others, and helped one another accomplish responsibilities. Again, their behavior and willingness to do so put another demand on me to rise up to the occasion and aim to become an example like this in my own American setting.

In a village where there are less distractions, less vehicles, fewer access to technology, and less of an addiction to social media or self-gratification, personal brands, and public images, I often wondered if the directive to share each other's burdens comes easier.

I've since come to realize that even if distractions in the Western world limit the time we can spend with others, there are other ways we can share in burdens. We can listen intently. We can help when a hand is needed. As I write this, we are in a global pandemic and I see many people volunteering to deliver food to the elderly or providing a helping hand to neighbors. For far too long, we've blamed our distractions and devices for our lack of friendliness and love, however, as believers, there are no adequate excuses for us to discount or disregard the only commandment in the New Testament that fulfills all of the laws of the Old Testament—that is to love our neighbors as we love ourselves. For far too long we've allowed distractions and excess to keep us from this important and vital part of life. If we are too inconvenienced, our schedules gravely interrupted, or we have to part with a material possession that is near to our hearts in order to meet another's burden or desire, we are not inclined to share that burden with them. It is easier to say, "Sorry I can't help you . . . I have to work . . . I have plans . . . That's out of my way . . . I have no time . . . I have a hair appointment . . . nail appointment . . . I promised my sister we'd go shopping . . ."

We have so many priorities, but do we ever stop to ask God, what is your priority? Perhaps he sends interruptions daily—opportunities for us to be his hands and feet, to meet needs in a heavenly way, but we are too consumed with the next agenda item or American luxury that we fail to discern the opportunities. We make friendship complicated when it is simple: to love one another and share others' burdens and to love in the way that Jesus modeled. Living in the village certainly tested and caused me to examine my own love walk and willingness to share in the burdens of others.

#4 Feasts and Friends

"And they devoted themselves to the apostles' teaching and the fellowship, to the breaking of bread and the prayers."

Acts 2:42

Sharing a meal together is one of the primary ways we build relationships, demonstrate respect, and show agreement with each other. In the gospels, after Jesus called Matthew, the tax collector to be his disciple, Matthew gave him a great feast in his own house (Luke 5:31), and there were a number of people there, including tax collectors, scribes, and Pharisees. This warm welcome with a feast and friends is a staple of East African cultures and many other cultures around the world. In Bulima, I was welcomed with so many meals during the first three months of my time there that I had gained about fifteen pounds by the time I ended my first missionary journey. I recall various occasions when I was eating lunch or dinner with a neighbor and other friends and neighbors would stop by and say hello, meet and greet, share their latest news, and ask me about life in America. Feasts and fellowship is certainly one way to give of ourselves and demonstrate love. Living in this culture put a new meaning on the phrase and popular book title by Keith Ferazzi, *Never Eat Alone.*

Of the countless meals I ate with families in Tanzania, I want to share the beautiful story of the meal myself and another missionary had on our first Sunday in the village. We ate with a third year student named Daniel, his neighbor Peter, and several of Daniel's children. Daniel had asked what we preferred to eat, and that morning he had gone fishing in Lake Victoria. For dinner, we had the most delicious fried fish I've tasted, fish soup with a tomato base, rice, gravy, and mango juice. There were two chairs in Daniel's home, which was a small, brick house that was identical to the dozens of other student homes. Most of us sat on the floor and ate. Daniel told us that his daughter Rebecca had just graduated from primary school at Simba Wa Yuda, and he wanted us to pray for her, read scriptures, and share encouraging words. We proceeded to read passages from 1 Timothy to her and each person spoke into her life about God's call and promises for her. Daniel then shared pictures and his vision for ministry. We spent close to three hours with his family that day enjoying a delicious meal and conversations. Afterwards, we took pictures and Daniel shared many of the challenges with being a missionary in Tanzania. Over the next five months, Daniel and his family were staples in my life and mission. I often ran into his beautiful daughter while walking through the village or preaching at nearby ministries. I even spent several hours of my last day in the village with two of his daughters, including Rebecca.

Food is a way of life in Tanzania. Relationships and bonds happen over meals. On many days during my first term in the country, I went home extremely full, almost sick because the family who hosted lunch or dinner insisted on me eating "more more." "There's still food left, Natasha." My first day in the village, the Kidds' invited me over to have dinner with their family of four boys. I also ate my last meal with them as well. Tanzanians say hello and goodbye over a good meal!

One week, the pastor's boys and first lady had come to my home after walking home with my neighbor and gave me a delicious piece of cake. A few days later, I decided to take their dish back, and the Mama was outside of the house cooking in the backyard. My plan was to drop off her dish and visit another neighbor. She, however, insisted that I sit so I could eat. She took me inside of her house and served me a delicious bowl of slightly salted potatoes and tomatoes. That soon became my favorite meal and I proceeded to eat lightly salted boiled potatoes with tomatoes almost every day for lunch for the next several weeks.

I realized that these encounters over food weren't only about food. They taught me new life skills I could use when I became a wife or a mother, skills that I took back to the States and used to serve my family members and friends who were in need of some TLC. I remember one of my friends telling me that his wife needed to know how to be a good hostess, and I later realized that every Tanzanian wife probably knows how to be a good hostess because that is what they do.

Leaving with More Life

God is so strategic in that nothing just serves one purpose and the full purpose of a moment or encounter may not be revealed until much later. Even now, I still receive many revelations about the life-giving moments I spent in the village, moments of learning new people and skills, trying new things and a new language, studying the Bible and the culture, teaching my students, and welcoming them to teach me.

When I returned home from Tanzania for the holiday, I remember sitting in a family member's home a few days before Christmas all alone. I only heard silence—no African music in the background, no birds chirping, or barking from Thunder and Micky. I couldn't hear the faint sound of a Swahili conversation in the distance, a mama digging in her shamba, or flip-flops and tires cracking along the rocky, dirt road. I felt empty and out-of-place. There was no one to talk to. No one was concerned about the long flight home or my friends and family in Christ in Tanzania. I missed *my* village. I missed the hodis from random school girls who wanted permission to pick my *matunda* (fruit) from the trees in my front yard. I missed the school boys standing on my porch repeating, "Madam . . . Madam. . . " On that cold, winter day as I sat in that quiet house overlooking empty land and bare tree branches, everything felt so empty and lifeless compared to the warm, vibrant life I had left behind in Tanzania. The people in Tanzania had given me themselves, and that was the best gift I had ever received. They had visibly shown me the meaning of Jesus' words recorded in John 15:13, "There is no greater love than to lay down one's life for one's friends" (NLT).

Life-giving Reflection and Journal:

As you read about the ways that the neighbors in the village give their lives, reflect on how your life aligns with some of the godly principles they demonstrated such as praying without ceasing, giving knowledge and wisdom, sharing in others' burdens, and spending time entertaining others with meals and fellowship? What are some ways that you can intentionally give your life in these ways to those in your circle? List them in your journal.

CHAPTER 19

cultural spiritual transformation

Notes from the Field

Lord, I thank you for today, this week, and this year. Before I start, let me just note that the WHO (World Health Organization) declared a worldwide pandemic because of the Coronavirus, which started in China and has swept all over the world to over 100 countries! 2 Chronicles 7:14. It's real. People are scared. Flights have been canceled. Schools have been closed. Universities are going totally online, and the (US) President has put a travel ban on Europe. I am scheduled to go home in three weeks and I am praying that this virus stops - so that I will still be able to get there. I have never seen anything like this.

—

Today was amazing. I taught the AIU Bible Interpretation class about interpreting parables and I showed them part 1 of "In the Dust of the Rabbi" . . .

Thursday, March 12, 2020
8:12 p.m.

One week later...

It's my last night in Bulima. Due to the Coronavirus, Rosemary and I have to leave. Today, when I was teaching my final AIU class of the term, Mwalimu Ndaro (the principal) came in and said all the students had to leave because the school was closing immediately. The government closed down schools in order to stop the spread of the virus.

God gave me so much grace this week and truly extended my time today and allowed me to visit with so many people. I gave away lots of clothes, so much food, and money and it felt good to be a blessing to my neighbors in the village. I feel so blessed and thankful.

I had lunch with Naomi's family and dinner at the Kidds'. I visited with the pastor's family, the Nungwanas, Nangales, and Daniel Kitundu's two daughters Rebecca and Rhoda came to visit me. They made me cards with notes and pictures and sat with me for a really long time. I gave them my nail polish, shoes, some shirts, English practice worksheets, and some vegetables from the garden. I then saw Nestory (the pastor's son, my little buddy), and gave him a book that I bought at a missionary sale in Mwanza.

Overall, it was a really blessed day. I'm so thankful. Now, I'm going to eat the last of my chocolate ice cream and lay down for bed.

Thursday, March 19, 2020
10:24 p.m.

Untimely Goodbye

On March 16, 2020, the first COVID-19 case was discovered in Tanzania. A 46-year-old woman had travelled from Belgium,

Denmark, Sweden, and into Tanzania by way of Kilimanjaro Airport. This same day, I learned that the Kenyan president announced travel restrictions, mandatory quarantines, and had prohibited non-Kenyan residents to enter the country. Over the next couple of days, the Coronavirus situation grew worse in the United States and Canada, and my missions agency grew more concerned with the short-term missionaries on the field. The following day, Tanzanian President John Magufuli closed schools, and I requested that my team inform me on the best actions to take. There were two more weeks remaining for me to be on the field.

I remember the day I learned I needed to leave. It was a Wednesday, March 18, and I had about thirty-six hours before I had to catch a rush flight out of Tanzania to Nairobi, Kenya where I'd be for a ten-hour layover before catching a six-hour flight to Qatar, and another four hour layover before my final half day flight to Dulles Airport in Virginia. The Wednesday that myself and Rosemary learned we had to leave the school was actually the final chapel service of the term, which meant it was an all-day prayer and worship program to close the academic term. An announcement was made in chapel and the students and teachers learned we had to leave early because there was a possibility that the borders would close. If that were to happen while we were still in the country, our short-term visas would expire and we'd be stuck in Africa illegally until the borders reopened. Rosemary was from Canada, and she only had just a twelve-hour window to pack, say her goodbyes, and leave.

For two months, I had actually been reading books about how to successfully transition out of cross-cultural service work, properly say good-bye to everyone on the field, and prepare for reentry into my home country. I had started mentally preparing for this emotional departure soon after I returned in January, but not even two months of preparation could have equipped me for this.

The novel Coronavirus (COVID-19) shut down our school and

disrupted the orderly exit strategy that I had designed in my head. Still, despite all of the unknowns, my last thirty-six hours in the village were some that I'll never forget.

At our farewell ceremony on Wednesday evening, we ate a big dinner, sat through several presentations, dancing, singing, and gift giving. Leaving Bulima was a bit traumatic, but even still, there was an outpouring of love from everyone I encountered. We were blessed that the farewell party had already been planned. In preparation for the party, the student council had dresses made for Rosemary and I. One of the student seamstresses sewed the most beautiful floral print matching outfits with raised, African style shoulders. Wednesday March 18 after prayer day concluded, many students came to our house to say goodbye. My neighbor entertained them with coffee and tea, we took pictures on the porch, prayed, and read Scripture. Naomi, one of my favorite women and students at the school came over with her husband. She asked for my Bible and began to read verses from Daniel 6 when God delivered Daniel from the lion's den. She encouraged me not to fear as I traveled home amidst a global outbreak of Coronavirus. Joyce, my favorite worship leader in Tanzania, came over to take pictures with me. Sarah and Aneth, the young ladies (who I call my girls) that I taught for three different courses and who helped me around my home on Saturdays came over as I had given them their pick of several items that I owned. This filled my heart with great joy.

At our farewell party that evening, we ate rice, chicken, mango, and drank chai chai. There was much dancing and Raphael, one of my amazingly talented students gifted in arts and crafts, made us both sashes with our names on them. As the entire school danced and sang, Mama Nangale, Mwalimu Kiula, Madam Edina, and Madam Mary, faculty members of the college danced and wrapped us in kitenge cloth. The students made signage wishing us farewell and blessings, and we sat in the front of the room at a long table with the school's principal, former church bishop, and our missions leader and associate principal, Abram. Students and teachers took turns saying words of encouragement, reading poems, singing songs, and we were able to share our last goodbyes. I made certificates for my advanced English tutoring group who sacrificed their Thursdays to study English with me.

The week or two before this all happened, I was laying in my bedroom, and I heard the Lord whisper to me, "Let some stuff go." When I heard these words in my ear, I initially thought it was a spiritual commandment telling me that I *still* had too much baggage. *Ughhh there goes that, "Pack light" lesson again.* At first, I felt like it was a command for my emotional well-being. Had I been holding on to too much baggage, too many feelings from the past, too much stuff preventing me to move forward? I am so quick to spiritualize things, and get all deep when God is sometimes very simple. I had been praying and seeking him for a breakthrough in my spiritual life. I had received so much in that area, and had grown a lot during my time in Africa. Little did I know, this was a practical directive that was for me but would impact my neighbors too. God was about to show me how, like Abraham in the book of Genesis, he had blessed me to be a blessing.

On Thursday, I felt like God truly gave me the grace of extended time. My heart was crushed because I felt like I was abandoning my post. Leaving my cherished village early, departing from the mission, saying goodbye to my students before we were done, and flying out of Tanzania without enough time to say my proper good-byes was crushing. So, I decided to have class on that last day even after the farewell ceremony because I felt the need to prepare my students for their final exams and impart some last minute prophetic words into their lives. This was the first of what I "let go." I thought highly of this class and I wanted them to know how special they are. This was the diploma class which had helped me in my home, who I mourned with over the course of six months as they lost two parents, the group that launched a story group with me, and listened to so many of my lectures pushing them to become who God called them to be. They were the group that I invested so much into. The ones whose ministries I'd visit on Sundays and who would ask for my advice on starting businesses. I had the honor of preaching at a harambee for one student in this class, an evangelist, who was raising funds for a ministry vehicle. This was the class who gave so much, and would volunteer to take videos and pictures whenever I preached. I had gifted them a copy of my first book and hosted them for banana bread and tea. It was also the group that I was tough with. Once, I caught a student plagiarizing on an exam and sadly had to reprimand this person and give them an F on the final. I desired for this group to search the Scriptures for themselves rather than rely on leaders to tell them what God said, and I told them that often. They meant a lot to me, so I was blessed to spend some treasured last moments with them.

Letting Go of the Excess

After the principal came into our final class and shut it down, the students and I took pictures outside, and I packed and walked with Naomi to her home, where we ate lunch: a freshly slaughtered and boiled chicken with rice and beans. Afterwards, neighbors came by to visit, and I slowly, but surely, gave away every physical item that I could from shoes and clothes to jewelry, food, beauty items, hair vitamins, my favorite dresses, and even some hair accessories. I felt like the Lord was operating through me as I emptied myself of the excess that had weighed me down on my flight to Tanzania. I didn't intentionally set out to give things away either. The Spirit took over and once it started, I couldn't stop. *"Let some stuff go."* This is what the Lord meant—become absent of excess in the natural and spiritual senses. It was one of the most beautiful days of my life. I was able to sit and talk with students who had become friends. The pastor's family came to help me around my house, and I gave them much of the food in the cabinet along with books. I ate dinner with the Kidd family, which includes my four favorite little boys in Tanzania. I gave away books and games, jewelry and shoes, clothes, food, spices, and much more. I laid down that night empty, yet filled with God's love. Filled with so many emotions. I couldn't believe that my time in the country was ending. I had become a part of that village and it was a part of me. I didn't know what America held for me when I returned and I honestly couldn't imagine my life there anymore.

I cannot properly explain or describe the impact that my neighbors in the village had on me. Some nights, I'd cry out to God because their kindness and love was unreal, unheard of, and yet my heart seemed so hardened and undeserving of it.

My time in Bulima had come to an abrupt end.

Notes from the Field Saturday, Flying over Greenwich, CT

I'm on the plane, the last leg of a two day journey home. . .

Although the mission was cut short by two weeks, and I still have so much to do in order to wrap things up, I feel good that I returned to Tanzania for nearly three months. It was a challenge being away from home for so long, and I had my moments of home sickness, loneliness, frustration, and irritations. Despite it all, I can say that I tried my best to teach well, spend time with God, love well, and properly steward the assignments and relationships both in Africa and in America.

(Here are my big personal takeaways.) I learned and God confirmed my identity: I have a passion and call for teaching. I connect well with young people. I am also designed as an entrepreneur and creative. Being in an African remote village for an extended period of time without proper internet and electricity connections definitely makes it quite challenging to do business. I realize that people value me, my smile, and the hope that I share through my words and stories. I can no longer be afraid to love and trust. I must let my walls and guards down. I love exploring new cultures. I hear from God. I need to keep early morning devotions and time with the Lord a part of my regular routine. I need to go to bed early so I can wake up early and spend time with God. I feel like I've grown so much in these past six months.

I want to do my best to bring home with me the lessons and positives I learned in Africa, especially the love and fellowship, and commitment to the Word. I do not want to get home and reconform to the culture there. I want to change the culture, make a difference, please God, and serve people. My heart has become filled with so much gratitude also and I'm overall just thankful for the experience, new friendships, opportunities, and impact that I've been able to make (with God in me). I'll miss hearing, "Hi Madam, Karibu!"

March 21, 2020
8:37 p.m. (Qatar Time)

Cross-cultural Travels and Service Change You

Spending a significant amount of time in a culture overseas, different from your own will change you. We often do not respect aspects of other cultures until we've truly understood them through cultural immersion. This is one reason why I was adamant about ensuring that my first experience as a cross-cultural missionary was one where I could stay for an extended period of time. Truth be told, when I first moved to Bulima, I really wanted God to confirm whether or not I was supposed to stay there for years or forever. I felt very little attachment to my life in the States and felt my gifts could have been put to better use in Africa. I wanted to make the most impact for God. While on the missions field, the Lord confirmed that I am designed to make an impact both at home and abroad, in business and in ministry. Although I am not fit to live in a village forever, I do believe God is calling me to long-term ministry in Bulima and who knows where else.

Living overseas makes you reconsider your values, morals, non-negotiables, and desires. While teaching theology, I underwent a spiritual transformation process. I learned a new language, new customs, and culture. I grew in my commitment to Christ and discipleship. I realized why Jesus told us to go into all the world to make disciples teaching them what he has commanded us (Matthew 28:18-20) and also why he told us to start local, then regional, and finally go global (Acts 1:8). Many people do not understand the case for cross-cultural missionary work, but the case is simply obedience to Jesus's command. He told us to engage the global community to win souls for him.

As a theological educator in Africa, I see why. In cultures where there is an absence of excess in monetary resources and educational access, there is often an absence of true apostolic teaching that aligns fully with Scripture. In many cultures there are beliefs mixed with Christianity that are far from what we learn in the word. My students have told me the stories that I plan to release in a future anthology about how they've had to fight spiritual battles with witch doctors and soothsayers who desired to convert them. For those who are privy to sound doctrinal teaching, our job is to walk alongside our brothers and sisters who need support so that they will be strengthened. For this reason, Christ gave the apostles, the prophets, the evangelists, the pastors, and teachers (see Ephesians 4). This is why global missions and true discipleship are necessary. We are called to build up the global body of Christ, not just our own areas. Every Christian is either called to pray for global missions work, give to global missions work, or go do global missions work. Go, pray, or send.

Every experience is different, but I can guarantee every experience will be life-changing.

We simply cannot begin to comprehend the ins and outs, victories and challenges of another culture, lifestyle, and Christian tradition until we experience life with the people as natives would. This process of learning, growing, engaging, and suffering with people on the opposite side of the earth taught me more about the patience and true love to which God calls us. It's taught me how to be content with less and see less for more. Parts of the world that are considered advanced are sometimes far less developed spiritually. I've learned to enjoy cooking and going to bed early. Spending time with God, after hours of serving others, has become my favorite time of the day.

Conclusion: Lessons from *The Absence of Excess*

In writing this book, I've realized how words often fail to do us justice. It's been difficult to put the experiences I've had into the right words that would resonate with someone other than myself.

I remember what I felt and what I saw, smelled, and how I initially reacted during each of these individual experiences. I can recall how deeply our neighbors in the stories within have impacted me and forever changed my perspectives. I know that words alone cannot begin to capture it all. Even photographs and pictures would not suffice. There are some lessons and major takeaways that I've stated in various parts of this book that I think it appropriate to reiterate now.

Lessons to Reconsider

1. God can often be found in simplicity.

2. Excess baggage weighs us down, both spiritually and naturally.

3. When we remove clutter, we experience clarity.

4. Even in the unknown, we can maintain peace if we focus on God.

5. We must welcome interruptions. They could be God-ordained.

6. The more hospitable we are, the more aligned with God's agape love we become.

7. We should partner in prayer for the food security of those in cultivation-based societies.

8. New single missionaries will have it tough; emotional preparation is required, but don't dare deny God's call.

9. Sometimes the longer (waiting) processes yield the best results.

10. God often draws us near to himself by challenging us to remove other voices.

11. We need the full manifestation of the Holy Spirit to operate in the power God has ordained.

12. Surrender what you think you need to receive what God wants to put in your hands.

13. Evangelism and outreach isn't convenient, but we must remain faithful in order for souls to be saved.

14. Purity in relationships makes divine partnerships easy to identify.

15. Children are blessings from God to their villages.

16. Jesus calls us to walk with others as they mourn.

17. As we humble ourselves and listen to others who seem to have less, we may actually gain and grow in areas that were blind spots.

18. God sets an example for giving which is giving our lives for others.

19. We may be economically different, but we are all made in the image of God, and in that we are all the same.

20. Cultural immersion takes dying to yourself for the sake of experiencing God's heart for the new place that he's placed you.

I pray that this book journey has been a blessing to you. I pray that the Lord has spoken to your soul and has prompted you to reflect. I am confident that as we become more aware of our excesses, God can shed us of all that's not necessary to experience him and love people the way he originally designed. As we live surrendered lives, we will become global citizens able to connect with neighbors around the world.

If you have read this book and have yet to receive the Lord Jesus Christ into your life or if you would like to recommit your life to Christ, please join me in speaking one last prayer. Say this prayer aloud. Allow the Lord to remove the baggage from your life and give you a new life in Christ. His Word says in John 3:16, "For God so loved the world that he gave his one and only Son, that whoever believes in him shall not perish but have eternal life."

Dear Father,
I come to you in the name of Jesus thanking you for speaking to my heart. I admit that I am a sinner. I have so much stuff in my life and I just want to be free. I want to be renewed, and I want to have a new life in Christ. I repent of every sin, and I ask that you would come into my heart Jesus and be my personal Lord and Savior. I believe that you died for me and you rose from the grave to give me a new life. Please remove the excess baggage and weight, remove the pain and torment, Lord fill me with your spirit. I receive you now Lord, in Jesus name, amen.

"After this I looked, and there before me was a great multitude
that no one could count, from every nation, tribe, people and
language, standing before the throne and before the Lamb.
They were wearing white robes and were holding palm branches
in their hands."

Revelation 7:9

discussion questions

1. How would you define missionary work?
2. What is the mission of God?
3. What is your current perspective of Africa in terms of the key issues raised in this book (Faith, Family, Economics, Religion, Cultural Practices, Agriculture)?
4. What new information did you learn?
5. Would you consider becoming a missionary? If so, where? What informs this decision?
6. Do you think it is important for Black Americans to serve in Africa? Why/Why not?
7. In what ways can you demonstrate godly love in a greater measure to those around you?
8. After reading the author's experiences and feelings, how would you respond to someone who thought they had to be the perfect Christian to serve God at home or abroad?
9. What are the effective biblical responses to spiritual warfare?

references

FOREWORD

Neely, Alan. "Liele, George." *Biographical Dictionary of Christian Missions*. Edited by Gerald H. Anderson, 400-1. New York: Macmillan Reference USA, 1998.

CHAPTER 5: BRIDE PRICES

African Studies Center University of Pennsylvania. "Tanzania Religion." *East Africa Living Encyclopedia*. Assessed September 9, 2020. https://www.africa.upenn.edu/NEH/treligion.htm.

Brown, Natasha. "Are there really black people in America?" Instagram TV, November 18, 2019. https://www.instagram.com/tv/B5BSFRzBFju/.

BBC News. "Bride Price Practices in Africa." Modified August 6, 2015. https://www.bbc.com/news/world-africa-33810273.

Dr. Y. "Bride Price Practices in Africa." African Heritage. January 5, 2018, https://afrolegends.com/2018/01/0/bride-price-practices-in-africa/.

CHAPTER 6: SINGLE, FEMALE, AFRICAN-AMERICAN MISSIONARY

AskaMissionary.com. "Are single women missionaries accepted in third-world countries? Married women without children?" Assessed August 15, 2020. https://www.askamissionary.com/question/564.

Engel, Elisabeth. "The (African) American Missionary Movement in Africa in the Early Twentieth Century." Process: A Blog for American History. August 29, 2017. http://www.processhistory.org/engel-american-missionaries/.

Killingray, David. "The Black Atlantic Missionary Movement and Africa, 1780s-1920s." *Journal of Religion in Africa* 33, no. 1 (2003): 3-31. http://www.jstor.org/stable/1581633.

Piper, John. "Why are Women More Eager Missionaries?" Desiring God Episode 982. December 28, 2016. https://www.desiringgod.org/interviews/why-are-women-more-eager-missionaries.

Stockton, Emily. "If Mr. Right Never Comes Along: A Single Woman on the Mission Field." IMB. September 5, 2017. https://www.imb.org/2017/09/05/single-woman-mission-field/.

CHAPTER 10: HOLY SPIRIT, COME

Liardon, Roberts. 1996. "Charles F. Parham—"The Father of Pentecost." *God's Generals: Why They Succeeded and Why Some Failed,* 121. New Kensington: Whitaker House, 1996.

CHAPTER 12: FAITHFUL OUTREACH AND EVANGELISM

Aduojo, Isaiah Negedu. "The African Predicament." Internet Encyclopedia of Philosophy (A Peer Reviewed Resource). Assessed September 10, 2020, https://www.iep.utm.edu/afr-pred/#sH2a.

Manji, Firoze and Yanguas, Pablo. "Should the West Stop Giving Aid to Africa?" New Internationalist. December 17, 2018. https://newint.org/features/2018/11/01/giving-aid-to-africa.

Moshi, H.P.B and Mtui, J.M. "Scoping Studies on China-Africa Economic Relations: The Case of Tanzania." Economic Research Bureau. Assessed September 10, 2020. https://media.africaportal.org/documents/Tanzania-China.pdf.

The World Bank. "Modest Reduction in Poverty in Tanzania: More Can Be Done to Accelerate Pro-Poor Growth." Press Release. December 11, 2019. https://www.worldbank.org/en/news/press-release/2019/12/11/modest-reduction-in-poverty-in-tanzania-more-can-be-done-to-accelerate-pro-poor-growth.

CHAPTER 17: THE WEST DOES NOT SAVE THE REST

Jones Jeffrey M.. "U.S. Church Membership Down Sharply in Past Two Decades." Gallop. April 18, 2019. https://news.gallup.com/poll/248837/church-membership-down-sharply-past-two-decades.aspx.

connect

If you enjoyed reading this book, please leave a review on Amazon.com or BarnesAndNoble.com. Consider purchasing copies of this book for your friends, family members, book clubs, and ministries.

To request the author for event, ministry, or media engagements, please contact

ELOHAI International Publishing & Media at hello@elohaiintl.com.

Visit ElohaiPublishing.com to get other books by Natasha T. Brown, including her bestselling book *10 Blessings of Betrayal: A Spiritual Journey of Rebuilding through Tragedy.*

Connect with Natasha T. Brown on Social Media:

Instagram @NatashaTBrown

Twitter @NatashaTBrown

YouTube @NatashaTBrown

LinkedIn @NatashaTBrown

Facebook @CommunicatorForChrist

Share your favorite takeaways or quotes on social media, and hashtag *#TheAbsenceofExcess*. Tag *@NatashaTBrown* and *@Elohai_Intl*.

To join Natasha in ministry events, including Bible Studies or prayer meetings, connect with the We Who Dwell Faith Community at www.wewhodwell.org or on Facebook. If you are in the United States, text DWELL to 55469.

A portion of the proceeds from this book will benefit students at Nassa Theological College in Bulima, Tanzania. If you would like to impact the community you have read about, please offer your support via the "Sow into Missions" link at natashatbrown.com.

biography

Natasha T. Brown, M.S, M.Div. is a minister, author, publisher, teacher, and missionary called to both business and global missions. For over fifteen years, she has partnered with organizations and individuals to share important stories as a communications consultant, publisher, ghostwriter and co-author of over twenty books.

In her role as a marketplace minister and global missionary, Natasha serves as the CEO of ELOHAI International Publishing & Media; founder of 10 Blessings Inspiration, Inc., a domestic violence support non-profit; and a prayer mobilizer for the We Who Dwell faith community, where she hosts a weekly prayer meeting and podcast called The Victory Prayer Circle.

In 2019, after graduating from seminary, Natasha began her work as a cross-cultural missionary and spent six months as a theological educator at Nassa Theological College in Tanzania. Her new book *The Absence of Excess* shares lessons from this journey.

Natasha earned a bachelor of science degree in communications from Morgan State University, a master of science degree in professional writing from Towson University, and a master of divinity degree with a concentration in marketplace ministry from Regent University.

Natasha is a survivor and advocate for abuse victims and survivors. In 2015, she published her first bestselling book *10 Blessings of Betrayal: A Spiritual Journey of Rebuilding through Tragedy* and was launched into the purpose of helping others share their stories through book publishing.

Natasha has been featured by numerous regional and national

media outlets, including *Black Enterprise Magazine* and was selected by General Motors to be a GM Influencer at the 2015 Stellar Gospel Music Awards. That year, she was also named a Forty Under 40 business honoree for Prince George's County, Maryland.

Today, Natasha T. Brown is focused on advancing the kingdom of God through discipleship, evangelism, Bible teaching, writing, and publishing important mission-centered stories. Connect with Natasha online at www.natashatbrown.com.